MW01234800

Courage to Flee:

Second Edition

Dr. Jeffrey A. Klick

What Others Are Saying:

"This book touches on a lot of key points that most people deal with on a daily basis. Being bombarded with social media and trying to conform to the norms of society by dressing, acting and being immodest, this book imparts wisdom that is truly priceless. Yes you will feel and will be portrayed as "different" for leading a moral life in an immoral world, but the knowledge gained in this book based on the authors experience and the word of God is far too important to ignore. Really, an excellent read and perfect for setting a good example for your children too!" - **A. Jenkins**

Courage to Flee brings a message that is so critical to the church in these days: moral purity is the answer to a world run amuck in perversion and selfishness. Morality's purpose is not to diminish our experiences in life—quite the opposite is true! Morality is God's way to enhance the joy and pleasure of God's design, and to prevent our souls from shriveling up and becoming poisoned through immorality. We are excited about this book! Breaking free from pornography, guarding against the immorality all around us and establishing authentic, God-designed intimacy are among the ways and means toward moral freedom! **The Intimate Couple.Com**

"Sex is everywhere in today's culture. You cannot turn on the television, go to a store, even leave your home without being confronted with immorality, immodesty, crudeness and vulgarity at every turn. How is a Christian or any decent person supposed to deal with this onslaught of temptation, this bombardment of sensuality, this assault on morality? Reading and following the Scripturally-based principles and teaching of *Courage to Flee* is one great way to handle the plague of lewd and licentious garbage that seeks as the Bible says, "to steal and destroy." The wisdom Pastor Klick shares will benefit both males and females in "living a moral life in an immoral world," the subtitle of this book. This is the kind of book in which you will want to be constantly underlining, highlighting, and starring. You will find yourself nodding in agreement and exclaiming, "Yes!" "That's right!" "Lord, help us!" I sincerely can not recommend this book highly enough. Every family should have AND READ a copy!" **T. Reads**

"Without knowing nothing more than my name and the fact that I like K-Love radio, a new co-worker of mine gave me this book when I coincidentally happened to be at a seminar at her Church with some friends (that neither of us knew we'd both be attending). She handed me this book unaware of anything I was currently facing in my life and this book was the RIGHT WORD in RIGHT SEASON! There is so much pressure, temptation and struggle around me as a young adult, Christian girl growing up in a sex driven, ungodly society. I've seemingly "failed" a lot in living a pure life, however, as Dr. Klick states in his book, "Failing doesn't make you a failure." God can redeem, restore and heal wounds from broken relationships and poor choices if we confess our sins, He's faithful and just to forgive them and part of repentance is turning AWAY from them. We are encouraged to FLEE sexual sins, which means to run as fast as we can away from them. This book gave me so much insight on boundaries to set in workplaces and even the marriage I hope to one day have. It let me in on some thought patterns of men, how to conduct myself in a manner that protects my brothers in Christ and things that I should be leery of if they are acting or presenting themselves to me in certain ways. This is a book I HIGHLY recommend." -**R. Wright**

"*Courage to Flee*" by Dr. Jeff Klick is a much-needed book in today's culture where lust and impurity are common-place. The book provides a strong biblical warning to those approaching the slippery slope of impurity, as well as great hope and practical counsel to those who have slid down its banks and are now entangled in the mud and quicksand of sin. This book should be in the hands of every pastor, as well as every man and woman who needs to know the biblical solution to freedom and purity."--**Mike Cleveland**, Pastor of Preaching and Vision, Ohio Valley Church and Founder and President of Setting Captives Free Ministry.

"I thought Pastor Klick should be commended for having the "Courage to Write this Book.". There are many books on the subject, but not many as concise and easy to read as Pastor Klick's. I appreciate the candor and humility that shows in *Courage to Flee*. Through reading this book, I realized that the time to instruct our children regarding moral purity is now--not when they are involved in a marital or personal problem. It is easy to forget to teach your children concepts, rather than construct rules to keep them on the "straight and narrow." Without understanding, I believe many will fall away from healthy personal habits. This book promotes that understanding. *Courage to Flee* would also be a good place to start for families new to the ideas of modesty and personal purity. Some of the concepts Pastor Klick explains will seem extreme to some folks. Thus enters the "Flee" part of *Courage to Flee*, because it *does* take courage to buck society and simply avoid certain things, for fear of moral failure. I believe that *Courage to Flee* lays down a challenge that, if taken up and crusaded, can help turn the tide of moral failure in our churches." **A. Hall**

"There is a lot of good discussion material in this book." Wonderful gems will be found in this book." "I loved this statement: "Being single is an opportunity to serve the Lord without distraction, and it is a waste to squander those years in frustration over not being married. That one statement provided enough discussion between my daughter and me to justify purchasing the book. I encourage families with young adults or children nearing adulthood to purchase *Courage to Flee*, read it, and then read it again with your older children." - **The Old Schoolhouse Magazine**

"I appreciate that this book was born out of a pastoral love for the local congregation. Far from other resources that seek to tear you down in order to build you up, there is encouragement on every page. The writing style is sermon-esque in that there are many visual illustrations, scripture references, and application. Still, Klick does not come off as preachy which is an accomplishment given the subject matter. His appeal to starvation is one of the better treatments on that "weapon" in spiritual warfare I have read. Chapter six on parenting your children is a must read. The conversational tone is much needed and makes the read enjoyable". **Christian Book Notes**

"Throughout his book, Pastor Klick uses appropriate scriptural references to encourage and exhort the reader. Personally, I am glad to see that he was not afraid to tackle any topic in the discussion of sexual immorality. Along the way, he uses his experience from over 30 years of marriage. Klick also shares from both success and failure, equipping the reader to know that they are not alone in this discussion. This review has been a long time coming. Actually, after receiving and reading my review copy, God immediately brought an individual into my life that could benefit from the content, so I quickly gave it away. Pastor Klick was kind enough to send a second copy to me, I doubt it will be in my possession too long. I highly recommend this book and would recommend that you buy a case at a time. Give them away to others, buy a copy for your pastoral staff, give them to a youth pastor...it's just that good!" **The Mango Times**

Scripture Translations:

The Holy Bible, English Standard Version Copyright © 2001 by Crossway Bibles, a division of Good News Publishers

New International Version (NIV) Copyright © 1973, 1978, 1984 by International Bible Society

New American Standard Bible (NASB) Copyright © 1960, 1962, 1963, 1968, 1971, 1972, 1973, 1975, 1977, 1995 by The Lockman Foundation

King James Version (KJV) Public Domain

Copyright Information:

No part of this publication may be reproduced, stored in a retrieval system, or transmitted in any way by any means—electronic, mechanical, photocopy, recording, or otherwise—without the prior permission of the copyright holder, except as provided by U.S.A. copyright law. Requests for permission should be made in writing.

Copyright © Jeffrey A. Klick, Shawnee, KS, 2013
All rights reserved

Acknowledgements

First, all glory and honor belong to Jesus Christ, for His wonderful gift of salvation and indescribable grace poured out on a sinner such as me. Second, I would like to thank my wife and family, who have steadfastly supported me through the good times and bad. Finally, for the graciousness of the members of Hope Family Fellowship, who provide support and encouragement.

Writing a book is typically a group task and this book is no exception. Many have contributed to this effort by being role models, editing, reviewing, and offering encouragement. May God richly bless you for the gift of life that you continuously give to me!

Published in January 2009, *Courage to Flee* was my first attempt at writing and was well received achieving both "Reader's and Editor's Choice" designations with the publisher. This revised edition has been expanded and now includes a study guide to help facilitate small group discussion.

I pray that the material presented will continue to assist many in the battle for moral purity. We can make a difference, and we can be free, if we will but start.

Introduction

Every journey begins somewhere.

Before becoming a Christian on July 25 1973, most people would have referred to me as a "hippy." Many days were spent in the pursuit of hedonistic pleasure, attempting to gain peace and happiness through immoral relationships, drugs, and music. God graciously intervened in that existence and brought me out of the kingdom of darkness into His glorious Kingdom of Light! For this, I am now, and eternally, grateful. In addition to His marvelous salvation, He brought a wonderful woman named Leslie into my life. We were married in May of 1975, and over the years, we marvel at what God has done for us. Neither my wife nor I came from a Christian home, and we had little training in how to have a godly marriage or how to raise children. God allowed us to attend a family-oriented training conference before we were married, and the information shared helped point us down a very different path from the one we had seen growing up.

By God's grace, we were able to stay married and to raise three children to adulthood. All three children have married and are walking with the Lord, and we have been blessed with ten wonderful grandchildren so far! Many authors, as well as some more mature couples, challenged us to train our children in a way different from that of the majority of people that we knew. While this book in your hands is not a child-training book, it does contain some principles that we used. All parents have struggles; we did and still do! Parents can teach, train, and pray; however, children must be humble enough to receive and then implement what their parents give to them. Please do not grow weary in your efforts!

As my wife and I were talking one day about some very serious issues regarding yet another couple dealing with immorality in their life, I had what I best could call "a flash of inspiration." In a moment's time, I knew I needed to write this book. Immediately, I arose and went down to my office and wrote out the chapter titles. Over the next few days, I filled in the material for each chapter. The words just flowed out, and I believe that God was leading as I typed. I trust that this book will be helpful in you and your families' quests for moral purity. My prayer is that the words written will stir something within you and help direct you down a different path. If it does, then God is the one to receive the Glory, for every good gift comes from His hand!

In 1982, when I first entered the ministry on a full-time basis, an older pastor took me aside and shared the occupational hazards of Christian service. Every job has its hazards and serving in the church is no different. If you are a carpenter, you can fall off a roof or cut off a finger. Airplane pilots can crash, and crane operators can tip over. This seasoned pastor said, "Jeff, there are four things that will take down a pastor and destroy his ministry: skirts, money, pride, and skirts!" At the time, I did not really understand the need to repeat "skirts." However, after all these years in ministry, it has become painfully clear what he meant. The pastor who shared this truth with me has since lost his ministry through adultery, and I have seen dozens of pastors "taken down" by skirts since those early years. It alarms me greatly. Why does this happen to men of God who are serving in the ministry? How could men who devote themselves to prayer and the study of God's Word throw out their families, their reputations, and their ministries for fleeting sexual pleasures? If they could fall, what hope do we have?

Regrettably, the problem is not isolated to those in full-time ministry. Christian counseling centers across the country are brimming over with marriages that are in trouble from infidelity, spouses trapped in pornography addiction, and teenage pregnancy issues. Human sexuality is not new or wicked, for God invented it. The devil, fallen humans, and our society have perverted it, and large numbers of people are being destroyed because of their failure to recognize this distortion. Many divorces occur because either the husband or wife has an affair. Vengefully, the other spouse has a retaliation fling. This unleashes waves of unforgiveness and bitterness; finally, the marriage falls apart.

Courage to Flee

As young people enter their sexual developmental age, experimentation follows, and parents are often the last ones to know. Abortions, sexually transmitted diseases, AIDS, and a host of broken lives follow. With Christian marriages experiencing skyrocketing divorce rates that rival the non-Christian statistics, and teenage rejection of their parents' faith soaring, is there any hope for the church, or will it simply follow in the same downward spiral as the society in which it lives?

Because of the easy access to pornography, millions are daily making an appointment with deception and destruction. A few simple clicks of a mouse and anyone of any age can enter what was formerly limited to some out-of-the-way dingy establishment deceptively called "adult entertainment." This exploitation of men and women unleashes havoc in the minds of those who engage in viewing. Pornography perpetrates unreal expectations upon its users; reality never matches the fantasy presented in these enhanced images. Frustration naturally follows, and striving after an illusion will often drive couples to the brink of despair. The perversion of what God designed cheats many out of the joy that the Creator intended.

As our society demands to normalize perversion, is there any hope left for followers of Jesus? Can the church survive? Will any marriages make it "until death do us part"? What hope does a parent have in our day to raise a pure son or daughter? How does a man or woman avoid the pitfalls of this ever-present temptation? How does someone who is already trapped escape? Can God still use me if I have already succumbed in the sexual arena? Is there freedom for those who are enslaved? Is it actually possible in our current sex-saturated day to have freedom from lust and moral failure? Can I be free from the guilt and shame of my hidden sins?

There is always hope, and some practical answers will be given in the pages to follow, so please do not give up. The picture is indeed bleak, but we serve a mighty God who has helped others, and He can provide healing, deliverance, and protection for those who seek it. We will never be completely free from temptation, but we can, and must, learn to walk in moral victory, saying "no" to the forbidden fruit. We can learn to control our thoughts, and we must learn to have the courage to flee from the snares of sexual immorality!

1. The Slippery Slope of Compromise

He who walks on ice carelessly, falleth quickly

I do not believe that someone wakes up one morning and says, "I think I will become addicted to pornography or commit adultery today." What typically happens is a much slower, more gradual process, involving a series of bad decisions. After the pastor I mentioned in the introduction left his wife and church, many asked me, "How could this happen?" My answer was, "The pastor made a series of small, wrong choices that took him where he should not have gone." Most of us are just one or two seemingly inconsequential compromises from ending up in a place we really do not want to be!

I remember as a youth encountering a person who was looking for trouble. I would draw a line in the sand or on the sidewalk and tell that person, "Do not cross this line if you know what is good for you." What I was telling that person was that if he or she crossed that line, there would be consequences! The reality was that many times the person would cross the line, and little happened, but crossing

7

moral lines is dangerous. God has drawn numerous lines and the person who ends up in moral failure has crossed a large number of them, ignoring God's provision for an escape. The scripture insightfully states:

> No temptation has overtaken you that is not common to man. God is faithful, and he will not let you be tempted beyond your ability, but with the temptation he will also provide the way of escape, that you may be able to endure it. (1 Corinthians 10:13)

When we say, "He fell into adultery," or, "She was overtaken by this affair," these are not altogether true statements according to the scripture. Upon a deeper examination of any immoral relationship, it becomes readily apparent that there were many opportunities to cut it off, or flee from it, but these were ignored or rejected.

What really happened was that a series of "lines" were crossed or compromised, and this ultimately led to the immoral relationship. Line after line was crossed, and deception was invited in and, ultimately, accepted. Rationalization soon followed, allowing the mind to be extremely creative in providing justifications, excuses, and blaming others for its own sin. In a later chapter, I will spell out some very clear boundaries that are necessary to survive in our culture, but for now let me touch on some of the issues that precede moral failure.

I heard a young, successful pastor proclaim to a large audience after an older pastor committed adultery, "I would never do such a thing," and a chill went up my spine. The arrogance of this statement was astounding and I have prayed that this young man would be able to live up to his boasting. There are certain things that we should have a healthy fear of, and moral failure is one of them. To think we are immune or unable to fall is naïve at best and extremely dangerous at worst. Of all the sins listed in the scripture, this type is one that we are told to run from.

Flee from sexual immorality. Every other sin a person commits is outside the body, but the sexually immoral person sins against his own body. (1 Corinthians 6:18)

To flee is defined as "to seek safety in flight," "to run away," and "to escape." What this means, in simple everyday language, is that a godly person needs to run for cover whenever he or she senses even a hint of sexual immorality arising in his or her life.

Long before someone ends up in a motel room or back seat of a car, many opportunities were provided to run away, but were suppressed or ignored. Addictions do not begin if they are never allowed to start. Addictions begin and grow with repeated feedings. There is a time to raise our shields of faith and boldly proclaim, "We will not move." Yet again, there is a time to know that we cannot win if we stay, and therefore we must run! The scripture tells us to run for our lives in the face of sexual immorality, and a wise person will heed this warning.

Humans tend to think that the problems or challenges we face are new or unique. The truth is that many in history have been trapped in marriages that were less than satisfactory, and young people have always faced sexual challenges as they have matured. Sexual temptation has been around since almost the beginning of time and even prostitution is glibly known as "the world's oldest profession." The struggles faced are real and often painful, but they are not unique, and our Heavenly Father knows them all. God loves us, and if we seek Him, He will provide what is lacking in our lives. He will provide a way out or through the dark, painful places we may be in.

People seek relationships with others for a variety of reasons, and many are righteous and valid, but all have an associated risk. Humans often attempt to substitute pleasure and human relationships for what only God can give. Since the beginning of recorded history, adultery and sexual perversions have been attempts to satisfy the need for love, acceptance, and self-worth. Ultimately, all have failed to satisfy, and all will continue to fall short, because the need can be met only in a personal relationship with our Creator.

The freedoms demanded and the quests for acceptance in our day from the sexually militant fringes of our society were present in Sodom thousands of years ago, and there are stories sprinkled throughout the pages of scripture dealing with immorality of all types. The issues that drive such behavior are real; they are just not new. The problem of immorality is ancient and so is the solution.

Compromise is defined in most dictionaries as "a concession to something detrimental." Another way to say it would be, "giving in to something that we know will eventually harm us." I entitled this chapter "The Slippery Slope of Compromise," and, in my mind, I have a picture of a hill covered with oil and someone sliding down it head first. We must use extreme care, for it is so easy to get into a lot of trouble in this area very quickly. Walking along the top edge with our eyes closed is foolish, and a slip is very likely, often leading to disastrous results. Many seem unaware of how slippery this slope is and how quickly one can slide into a mess. One or two "concessions" can speedily take us down the hill. We must be aware of where we are, and what we are doing at all times, to avoid a painful spill. Not recognizing the danger, or being ignorant of our potential to fall, places us in the category of being "simple."

The prudent sees danger and hides himself, but the simple go on and suffer for it. (Proverbs 22:3)

Most of us know the old saying, "If you play with fire, you will get burned." Many of us have relational scars that we received from not heeding this warning. Experience may be an excellent teacher, but it is not the best or only way to learn. Those of us who are scarred from playing with fire plead with those yet unmarked to flee the flames! Become a prudent man or woman and hide yourself from the dangers discussed in this book! Learn from others who bear the marks of foolish choices. You do not have to be burned if you never play with fire in the first place.

Examine the lives of men in the scripture who were trapped in immorality and learn from their choices. David, Solomon, and Sampson would all be excellent studies to begin to understand the scars that are earned by playing with sexual fire. Eyes were lost and kingdoms destroyed because these men did not flee from temptation. In our day, one does not have to search too hard to find men of God who have fallen into shameful behaviors and lost thriving ministries. If we could learn from observing others, we could avoid a great deal of pain and heartache.

God designed men and women to be attracted to each other and ignoring this fact is like standing on the top of that hill, covered with oil, blindfolded. I am not a psychiatrist, sociologist, or any other "ist," but a pastor who has spent the better part of his life attempting to help people who have taken a tumble down that oil-covered hill because they did not understand basic human nature. I am not a math major either; however, I do understand one formula very well:

Men + women in close proximity for extended periods of time will very quickly = a major potential problem.

The attraction will be different from the male and female vantage points, but the root problem is the same. God designed men and women to be attractive to each other and our history has proved this true. Given this undeniable fact, we must be careful, we must take precautions, and we must be prepared to deal with it in a righteous manner.

Compromise begins for a pastor when he spends time alone with a woman other than his wife. Counseling, praying with and for someone, talking on the phone, and offering protection and spiritual leadership are all acceptable practices for a pastor, while being a recipe for disaster if they are not balanced out with some common sense.

A pastor should not take the place of the husband or father, and a man is foolish if he allows himself to be placed in this position. I will explain in more detail later how to set up acceptable guidelines to help, but the pastor needs to make sure his motives are right and pure before God whenever he is talking with a woman who is not his wife. Pastors are people and are therefore subject to the same temptations, desires, and lies as all other humans.

Women trapped in unhappy marriages often idolize and fantasize about their pastors, so we must be extremely careful when we interact with those women. The pastor who only attempts to control or deny his emotions in the face of sexual temptations, instead of fleeing, will probably fail. Our newspapers and news outlets are littered with many stories of such failures of men of God who did not flee. The damage caused by these moral failures have crippled and destroyed many successful works across our nation, and only God knows the damage caused to the sheep by the failure of the undershepherds. While not venturing into the theology associated with salvation, many have rejected Christ and blamed the sexual failures of these ministers as their reason for rejecting Christianity. I believe we will give an account someday of what we have done before our Lord. If we fail sexually, we will have to explain to the Ultimate Purity why we chose to pursue impurity.

The attraction between male and female is so strong that it is unwise for men and women who are not married to have close friendships or repeated interactions with people of the opposite sex. Are you saying that couples should not be friends with other couples? No, but they should be friends *as* couples. A husband who has an intimate relationship with another man's wife is heading for trouble and vice versa. Spending time alone with someone of the opposite sex who is not your spouse opens the door to thoughts and temptations that you should not allow in. I have known many couples who destroyed both their marriages by not following these cautions.

For example, one woman began to ride on the back of a motorcycle with her friend's husband. Soon they found many interests in common and the rides became more frequent. Instead of holding the bar on the seat, it was perfectly natural to hold on to the driver. It was not long before both marriages were destroyed. Bonding through frequent communication begins quickly and is extremely difficult to un-bond. Why do an estimated 85 percent of affairs occur in the workplace if this is not true?

Why do so many who participate in the theater end up in relational difficulty? I am not opposed to the arts, but people are simply not thinking properly if they do not realize that intense communication, physical contact, and extended time together between male and female can lead to disaster. Common sense would dictate that kissing, touching, and lovingly looking into someone of the opposite sex's eyes can lead to trouble, even if the participants are only "acting." We are all familiar with the swapping of mates common in Hollywood but seem to ignore the possibility and temptations in Christian productions.

A large church had an annual Easter production that was the envy of the city. Each year hundreds of people would volunteer to make this production spectacular. Men and women would spend at least four months giving large chunks of their time, often late into the night, preparing for the production. Is it any wonder that, just about every year, affairs took place and marriages ended up being destroyed? Spending hours in conversation with, pursuing a common goal, even a spiritual one, or touching someone other than your spouse places you on the top of the oil-covered hill. We must take off our blindfolds and carefully descend from this dangerous place before we find ourselves tumbling down headfirst out of control!

How does someone end up in an emotional entanglement or a physically immoral relationship while professing the Lordship of Jesus? It begins with compromise and line crossing and continues with ignoring the opportunities to flee temptation provided by God.

Courage to Flee

In the next chapter, we will examine how our thinking ultimately leads to action, but before moving on, stop and consider some of what was written in the first chapter. Prayerfully think about the questions in the Study Guide and take whatever action is necessary to keep yourself morally pure.

2. We Do What We Think

A mind is a terrible thing to waste on sin

In the early days of computers there was an acronym, "GIGO," which meant "garbage in, garbage out." What the programmers did not realize was that they were simply quoting scripture. In The King James Version, Proverbs 23:7 begins, "As a man thinketh in his heart, so *is* he." Thinking precedes action. What we feed upon or allow in our thought life will eventually bring forth fruit in our actions or changes in our behavior. If we are filling our minds with truth, then truth will come out in our actions. If we are filling our minds with error and deception, then our behavior will eventually follow this path. If we learned to deal with our sexual or sensual thoughts in seedling form, they would be much easier to control.

I am not much of a gardener. In fact, I practically have two black thumbs when it comes to growing plants and flowers. However, I can grow weeds in abundance! What I have discovered is that removing weeds when they are small is much easier than

17

attempting to dig them out when they have had time to grow long, strong roots.

We do not have much control over what thoughts pass through our minds, but we can determine what we invite in to visit and allow taking root. My mind is very active and, frankly, much of what goes through it has to be rejected quickly. Temptations begin in the mind and much of the battle is won or lost in the early stages of the struggle. The scripture gives us some insightful directions:

We destroy arguments and every lofty opinion raised against the knowledge of God, and take every thought captive to obey Christ. (2 Corinthians 10:5)

Do not be conformed to this world, but be transformed by the renewal of your mind, that by testing you may discern what is the will of God, what is good and acceptable and perfect. (Romans 12:2)

The battle for our sexual souls rages between our ears, resting squarely in our minds. Over the years, many men have shared with me some of their typical battles. For example, a scantily clad young woman walks into a man's line of sight, and a flood of thoughts begins to flow. An image pops up on another man's computer screen, tempting him to linger, or inviting him to find a soul mate in his city, and his mind wanders. Multiple images from dating services promoting beautiful women that are looking just for him end up right before his eyes on his computer screen. Cheerleaders, swimsuit ads, and a plethora of other visual stimuli are presented continually, and a man's thoughts need very little encouragement to go in a destructive direction.

Men and women fantasize differently, I am told, but the battles are very real and the solution is the same. Whether the temptation is physical in nature or emotional, it is still an invitation to sin and disaster, so the thoughts must be dealt with early and decisively.

My thoughts need to be controlled, taken into obedience to Christ, and not given free reign to run wild. My mind desperately needs to be purged and renewed by the Word of God, daily. I need to be so familiar with truth that lies become obvious, and I may quickly reject them. Instead of taking my lustful thoughts captive by comparing them to Jesus and His Word, I sometimes pull up a chair and invite them in for a nice, long chat. I should be appalled by them, rejecting them and casting them out.

When we become hospitable to destructive thoughts, we fail. There is a proper time to be rude and, when sexual temptation is knocking on the door, it would be wise to ignore it! Every thought needs to be tested and if it is not in line with God's Word or moral purity, it needs to be rejected before we allow it to take root in our hearts and minds and eventually act upon it.

Being tempted is not the same as sinning. Jesus was tempted with lust. Does that shock you? It shouldn't. If Jesus was tempted in all things just like us, (Hebrews 4:15) then He had to be tempted with lust. Maybe the woman at the well was beautiful. She must have been pretty nice to look at because she had been with five different men. Maybe Mary Magdalene was gorgeous. We don't know, but if Jesus was a real man, and He was, if He was totally human, and He was, then He had to deal with the same lustful temptations we deal with, yet without sin. The point is not what Jesus dealt with, but that temptation is common to all men and just because you are tempted, does not mean you have sinned. What we do in *response* to the temptation determines if we sin or not.

Long before you meet another for an illicit encounter, your mind has been actively engaged. Thoughts that you should have rejected quickly have been entertained and eventually given a place in your consideration. Whatever ultimate justification you use to explain the sinful behavior, it began in your mind with something like this:

- My spouse is not meeting my needs physically or emotionally, so this behavior is necessary and justified.
- I married the wrong person and if I divorced her (or him), I could marry someone else who would be the right one for me.
- I am not hurting anyone by my behavior so it is fine.
- The one I hear the most: "God wants me happy."

Underneath these sentences is a great deal of thought, most of which is incorrect and dangerous. In the first one, your needs *should not* be the driving motivational issue; laying down your life for others is supposed to be. Next, you are responsible for your own actions and reactions, not your spouse's lack of responsiveness. You cannot change your husband or wife in any fashion; what you should be asking is, "What can I do differently to help and serve my spouse?" You should be asking if you are meeting *his* or *her* needs; how you can lay down your life for your spouse. Being focused on your own needs is an unbiblical pattern that typically ends in disaster.

While the second statement may be partially true, it is still a lie. Once you were married, your spouse became the right person! Dumping your spouse in the hopes of finding a better one will not be successful because you are still part of the equation. Once you said, "I do," you did. You probably took vows before God and others and said something along the lines of, "Till death do us part." If you are reading this, you are most likely not dead yet, so reneging on your vows is not an honorable option. If you divorce and marry another, you will simply have to learn what you failed to learn in the current marriage. You will not avoid the lesson needing to be learned by changing partners; you will simply have to start all over again.

"I am not hurting anyone" is also in error, for no sin happens in a vacuum. If you are married, you are hurting a large number of others by your immoral behavior. If you have children, family, or friends, they are all going to be affected by your sinful choices. If there are those who know you are a Christian, you are hurting your testimony and the cause of Christ.

The final one, "God wants me happy," is unbiblical and self-absorbed. God promises joy in spite of difficult circumstances, but happiness is a choice we make and we will experience neither joy nor happiness when willfully sinning. God wants us holy, mature, content, and serving others, and true happiness will come from these, not from immorality or self-focused behavior.

People frequently say, "Well, no one knows about it so it is fine," this also is an illusion. At least two know at all times. First, you are painfully aware of it, and are therefore hindered by your sinful actions with the accompanying guilt, hardness of heart, or fear of discovery. Second, God knows, and your relationship with Him is being strained as you persist in rebellion. A saying I read, but can't remember where, stated,

> *"Sin will always take you further than you wanted to go and cost you more than you ever imagined."*

Almost everyone who ends up in immorality comes to a place of regret. Families are destroyed. Reputations, which took years to build, are crumbled in minutes. Trust is lost and guilt ensues that is staggering. What seemed so pleasurable and worth the risk earlier now is revealed for the lie it was. The wages of sin is death and they are always paid.

I have asked this question many times to various groups and I present it here for your reflection:

"Is it better to avoid temptation or to overcome it?"

Of course, the answer will vary depending on the nature of the temptation and your available options, but for me, avoidance works every time, whereas overcoming sometimes does not. Regarding sexual sin, it is far better to never have to flee from an intensely emotional, stimulating encounter in the first place, then to overcome it in the middle of the fire. In most cases, once the hormones have become engaged correct thinking is difficult.

How do I know if a particular activity or thought is harmful to me? Glad you asked! Here is a "filter" that can be used to test what you are reading, viewing, or thinking about:

> *Finally, brothers, whatever is true, whatever is honorable, whatever is just, whatever is pure, whatever is lovely, whatever is commendable, if there is any excellence, if there is anything worthy of praise, think about these things. (Philippians 4:8)*

If the book, website, TV program, video, game, chat room, etc. can be "filtered" through this verse then it is most likely a worthy endeavor. For the record, pornography, flirtation, adultery, immorality, sexually suggestive material in any form, and most fantasies will not pass unchallenged through this test!

What I feast on nurtures or deprives my mind and spirit, and will lead me either closer to God, or in some other direction. If I feed my mind with the world's sensually oriented materials, I can expect to develop lust and to struggle with impurity in my thought life. On the other hand, if I fill my mind with godly literature, the Word of God, wholesome entertainment, and non-sensually-oriented music, my thought life will be easier to manage. GIGO is as true in our minds as in our computers.

In the next chapter, I will get a little more specific about how what we see influences what we think. The scripture states in Matthew 6:22, "The eye is the lamp of the body," so what we focus on with our eyes influences what fruit we produce in our lives.

3. The Eyes Are the Window to the Soul

Where has all the fabric gone?

I do not go to malls if I can help it, and it is not the pain of shopping that bothers me; I cannot endure all of the skin that is being presented to my eyes. Please, do not misunderstand me; it is not that I do not like the way women look. The problem is I am male and I like it too much. The malls in my city are full of giant pictures of partially dressed women, and the walkways are populated with girls of all ages desperately attempting to imitate the images being presented. For a man desiring to control his thought life, malls are a dangerous place.

I also shun public pools and our local amusement park that contains a giant beach for the same reason. I have often wondered why a woman who would be greatly embarrassed to be accidentally seen in a full-length slip in her front yard can wear a tiny bikini without fear. Is it the fact that her bikini is purple and has a starfish on it? The frenzy to expose as much of the female body as possible is simply more than I care to resist, so I limit my exposure to it whenever possible. You may think, "That's such a coward's way out," and I would agree with you. I am afraid, very afraid. It is not the women that scare me, but my own wicked, sinful desires. I would rather avoid temptation than overcome it.

I believe our eyes are under constant sensual assault everywhere: TV, sporting events, billboards, Internet, computer games, magazines, and just about anywhere anything is being sold. Sensual advertising is used to sell almost any product, including clothes, cars, liquid refreshment, and even children's toys. It is difficult to enter almost any store and not be confronted with underwear ads, slinky clothing, sexually oriented mannequins, and sexual pleasure-enhancing products. It is frustrating to watch sporting events for the same reason. The games are constantly being supplemented with cheerleaders and beer commercials that seem to be competing to see how little clothing can be worn and still avoid fines from the FCC.

Our culture is almost completely given over to sensuality and perversion, and it seems that many in the church are not too far behind in acceptance and imitation. As a pastor, I have a confession to make. I almost hate doing weddings these days. Most pastors and laymen who have confided in me speak of intense struggling with their thought lives at weddings due to the exposure of flesh that is now generally accepted as normal. The dresses that are in style are very tight and revealing and almost a constant distraction, and I am not even talking about the wedding party!

The dresses being worn today by godly women of all ages are disappointing at best and shocking at worst. Cleavage abounds and it seems that the preferred fashion is for the clothing to be so tight that everyone can tell how many moles someone has though the fabric. The Christian folks compare what the world is wearing to their fashions and seem to think, "I'm not that bad." I believe that is the wrong standard. Nude beaches and cruises are becoming quite normal for the world; will the church join in these shortly? Somewhere we must draw lines of acceptability. We are not to imitate evil but to overcome it with good.

Every once in a while, I turn on the Disney channel just to see what is going on in our youth culture. One pattern I notice is that even young children are encouraged to dress sexily, and that physical appearance is a primary focus of attention. Pre-pubescent girls are encouraged to dress as if they were in their late teens or early twenties. Young men who should be playing with army men or bugs are now following these girls around with their eyes glazed over, and this picture is presented as normal. After years of these images being presented to our children, is there any wonder that teen-aged promiscuity becomes the normal way of life?

Many surveys reveal the shocking facts that young people are experimenting sexually at younger and younger ages, yet many do not make the obvious connection. The young people are simply acting out what they have been taught through the messages being repeatedly presented to them. Sex and sensually oriented behavior is clearly presented as the normal behavior, so why are our society and the church shocked when the young people implement what they have been trained to do?

Again, this is not really a new problem, but a very old one. Sensuality and immodesty have been with us since the very early stages of human development. Women have always known that what they wear, and how they wear it, has an impact on men. Throughout the pages of scripture, there were women who were referred to as harlots and prostitutes and usually the connection was made to how they were dressed.

- Judah thought his daughter-in-law was a prostitute because of how she was dressed. (Genesis 38:15)
- Sampson went to Gaza and saw a prostitute, and we all know how that ended, with a very bad haircut! (Judges 16:1)
- "And behold, the woman meets him, dressed as a prostitute" (Proverbs 7:10)

King David was walking on his roof when he should have been off to war. He glanced over at the next rooftop and beheld a woman taking a bath. The Bible does not really say, but Bathsheba apparently did not grab a towel to cover up and she really did not seem to resist too much when David sent for her. David should have fled instead of inviting destruction into his bed. Sad poetry, I know, but nonetheless true. David was trapped by what he saw. The power of seeing a woman's body overcame any rational or spiritual thoughts by "this man after God's own heart," so are you and I immune?

What we look at and how we react to what we see will have an impact on how we behave. Those who study such things say that men are stimulated by what they see much more than in any other way. If "the eye is the lamp of our body," as Jesus stated, what "light" are we allowing into the room in our mind?

If we allow ourselves to examine every female body we encounter, is that helping our thought life and helping us walk in moral purity? Watching sensual movies or visiting websites that contain stimulating images of the opposite sex will not help us in our battle to control our thoughts. What we let our eyes feast upon will either help or hinder our thought lives. What our "windows" open to will determine the quantity and quality of light we have in our lives.

Most men understand the "law of second glance." If you have not encountered that phrase, let me explain it to you. Often I have no control over what comes into my line of sight. However, I do have a great deal of say over how many times I look at it! As a man who is not blind, I cannot help but notice an attractive woman. Up to this point, I have not sinned, or crossed any illegal lines, by simply noticing her. Enter the law of second glance. What do I do now that I have seen her (or a picture)? An interesting exercise is to watch a man's eyes when you are out to a meal with him. Notice what he looks at and for how long and you will gain a glimpse into his soul.

Courage to Flee

The eyes are a window to give us a bit of insight into the mind. I cannot help but look once, but any more than that and I have crossed a line that is not helpful to me in my desire to be a man of purity. Over the years, I have had men attempt to rationalize their behavior in this area. "I simply appreciate God's creative genius," one told me. "That is why I stare at women." "I can look at all the skin I want and it does not impact me," boldly proclaimed another. "God created nakedness and so there is nothing wrong with me looking at women," shared a third. While there is an element of truth in each statement, there is also a significant amount of deception and self-delusion. God is very creative and there is nothing wrong with skin and nakedness in the correct situation. God's Word leaves little doubt about the correct realm for this arena of enjoyment, and it is called marriage. Perhaps there really does exist a man that can stare at all the skin and women he wants without lust or temptation; I simply have never met him.

Our God is a redeeming God and we do not know what would have happened in David's life if he had not taken that second look over at the other roof. We know what did happen: adultery, murder, a divided family, a rebellion of a favorite son, and an unleashing of death that plagued David and his family until the day he died. God did redeem the mess so much that Bathsheba ended up being part of the bloodline of Christ, but I am pretty sure that God could have accomplished the same thing without all the misery that David caused by his sin.

The people with whom I have interacted over the years who did not flee from temptation in the sexual arena also experienced death, not quite as gruesome as King David's, but death nonetheless. Families were destroyed, rebellion arose in their offspring, who often rejected their parent's faith, and the children were emotionally scarred for decades; these results are all quite normal when immorality is allowed to rule. God is redemptive, but the cost is enormous when we fail sexually.

Jesus' complete thought in Matthew 6:22-23 is:

"The eye is the lamp of the body. So, if your eye is healthy, your whole body will be full of light, but if your eye is bad, your whole body will be full of darkness. If then the light in you is darkness, how great is the darkness!"

Darkness can enter our souls though our eyes, so what we allow our eyes to dwell on affects the amount of light in our life. If the light that is in us is dark, we are in trouble. If I feast on flesh and let my mind run wild in fantasies, darkness increases its grip in my heart.

Lust and sexual desire have similar attributes to fire. I have been burning wood for three decades and never has the fire ever told me to "stop, I do not need any more wood to burn." Instead, more is needed and always desired. The same is true with lust. I have been told that the sex drive in men is the second strongest drive possessed by males, just behind the will to survive. I cannot prove

31

this; however, I am inclined to agree. When attempting to explain this drive in men to women I have found this word picture to be helpful. A certain religion in our world promises men the opportunity to spend all of eternity with seventy virgins if they die in a particular fashion. I have yet to meet a woman who wants to spend all of eternity with seventy men! These men are willing to strap bombs to their bodies in order to be blown up for the chance to have a personal harem. I do not think these men want to have seventy women for eternity simply to ensure that there is always someone around for a good conversation. The potential for unlimited, eternal sex compels many of these men to take their own lives. Lust is never satisfied and, once unleashed, it is very difficult to contain.

Jesus said that His people were to be "children of light." If we are trapped in lust and immorality, we are living in darkness and our lamps are in danger of being put out for good. We are to be "lights on the hill" and "not hide our lamps under a basket." If what we are looking at is producing darkness instead of light, "how great is that darkness!"

What if you are already entangled in lust or pornography; is there any way to escape? Are there any insights on how to resist this sensual world and its powerful draw? Is there still hope for those who have already given in to lust or immorality? In the next chapter, I will begin to outline some helpful suggestions for how to survive in our perverse world and escape from the enemy's snare.

4. Help for the Entangled: How Do I Escape?

Do not start down the wrong road and you will not end up in the wrong place

The guilt floods in after the screen goes black. In spite of your passionate promises to yourself and God, you went back to that website or turned on that late night TV show. It seems no matter how hard you try, you just cannot help yourself when you are around that person at work. Thoughts flood into your mind and though you know you should resist them, you find yourself wondering about the life you could have with your co-worker yet again. The thoughts begin, and before you know it, you are fifteen minutes into a fantasy and you wonder, "How did I get here?"

Does any of this sound familiar? If you have not experienced it personally, I can assure you there are plenty of Christians who deal with any or all of these issues daily. Many more have taken those thoughts and acted upon them and are currently involved in immoral relationships, or perhaps visiting so-called "adult" clubs or websites.

Some begin relationships via seductive chat rooms and flirtations that often lead to encounters in cars and motels.

If you are trapped in an immoral relationship, or bound by a damaging behavior, or heading down a path of destruction, there is help for you if you desire it. God still loves you, and He will give you the strength to change if you return to Him. God is the ultimate prodigal's Father; He is waiting for you to come to the end of yourself and run to Him.

Our enemy lies to us and tells us that God wants nothing to do with us, but this is absolutely false. God's throne is surrounded with thunder and lightning, and with majestic beings beyond our wildest imaginations, but it is primarily known as a place to receive grace and mercy in our time of need! (See Hebrews 4:14-16) God wants us to run *to* Him, not *away* from Him, especially in this arena of sexual struggle. He is not shocked or appalled by our failures. He loved us when we were His enemies; does He love us less as His children? He loves us and understands us and we must go to Him.

"If you keep doing the same things you have always done you will keep getting the same results you have always gotten," goes the famous truism. In over thirty years of dealing with people who are trapped in lust, pornography, and immoral relationships, I have found only one effective long-term cure—starvation. Feeding lust with additional images and discussions will only produce more lust. There is no such thing as a little lust. The desire to view pornography will never be satisfied. Catalog images of women in underwear give way to semi-naked swimsuits; swimsuits give way to semi-nude pictures. These move the viewer on to fully nude photos and in due course to movies or live action shots. Eventually, pictures and movies will not satisfy this lust so human contacts are sought out, and the one now trapped wonders, "How did I get here?" You got there in small steps, but the solution requires a big one—starvation. You must resist the urge to look at these types of pictures or movies from now on! Starvation is effective every time it is used.

The images that are imprinted in your mind will stay and often resurface, but if you do not add new ones, you can learn to deal with the old ones more effectually. The medical community labels alcoholism as a disease. What is interesting to me is that there are tens of thousands of distribution centers all over the country for this disease, including most restaurants, bars, and grocery stores. What has been discovered is that this disease can be controlled, conquered, or even avoided completely, simply by never taking the first drink. Starvation works every time.

The same is true for lust and immorality. In the same way someone overcomes an alcohol addiction, a lust addiction can be defeated. A drunk must never take another drink, ever. A lust addict must not feed the addiction with additional images, ever. We must be aware of how quickly we can fall, and do whatever is necessary to prevent it in order to win this battle! This is a war and war demands strong, decisive action.

If you are attracted to someone to whom you are not married, avoidance is the only effective solution. A woman called me and said, "I am considering an affair with a co-worker who is a

Christian; what should I do?" My answer was somewhat shocking to her, I think, but I told her to quit her job, and do it today! As long as you are in his presence, and can be in contact with him, you will never be free of the fantasy. Whether or not the man really was a Christian is beyond the scope of this book, but rest assured, if you are attracted to someone, or worse, involved with someone, at work, fleeing is the only solution. It is practically impossible to be involved with someone emotionally or physically and not be tempted when you remain in close proximity. Starvation is the only 100-percent-effective solution. Out of sight out of mind will eventually work, but you first must get the person out of your sight to keep him or her out of your mind!

Starvation works every time for sensual TV shows, videos, books, chat rooms, and Internet pornography. I am not promising that you will not be tempted, but I can assure you that if you keep feeding whatever issue you are dealing with, you will never get free from it. Drastic problems require drastic action. Throw out the TV or remove the Internet. Quit your job or burn the books, change churches or move out of town, but whatever it takes, freedom is worth the expense. Your relationship with God, your family, and your testimony to a lost and dying world are worth any price to be free from the chains of lust and immorality!

As I mentioned before, it is deception to believe that when you commit this type of sin, no one else is getting hurt. Nothing could be further from the truth! If you are married, your spouse is being hurt by the violation of your wedding vows. The trust you are destroying will be extremely difficult to recover. If you have children, they will suffer for the rest of their lives due to these types of sins. Children need heroes, and parents are supposed to fulfill that role. When your children discover or understand the lying and deceit that has taken place, the fall of their hero will shake them to the very foundation. Losing the trust, love and respect of your spouse and children is a huge price tag for a few minutes of fleeting pleasure.

Sexually immoral parents provide a role model for their children to become sexually immoral. In addition, when everything finally is exposed, and rest assured it all will come out some day, your personal testimony is ruined. Think of all the damage caused by the well-known Christian TV personalities who have been exposed for their sexual transgressions. These ministers of the Gospel thought that they could sin without being found out. Yet, their sins end up being shouted (broadcast) from the rooftops! The testimony of Christ has been scorned at the national level due to these men's participation in immorality, and, frankly, non-Christians have the right to mock. The charge of hypocrisy rings true when we live the lie of immorality.

Beyond all of this, when we sin, we sin primarily against God. By using His grace as a license to gratify our flesh, we have not lived up to the gift we have been given in salvation. Paul challenged the Philippians in 1:27, "Only let your manner of life be worthy of the gospel of Christ." When we fail morally, we are not living worthy lives. In addition, our relationship with God suffers when we willingly sin. Giving into lust and immorality is a sin against God and we must begin the healing process right here.

One wise pastor used to tell me, "Viewing pornography is like having a quiet time with the devil!" Believers should be spending quiet time with God, not with the father of lies. Lust, pornography, and immorality are all lies that promise satisfaction, yet deliver only more craving, death, and despair, and numerous people are severely impacted by this behavior. The devil states, "You are not hurting anyone." Seems he said something like that to Adam and Eve as well.

As with any other sin, the solution begins with repentance. Repentance in its root form means to turn around, or away from. Literally, it is to walk in a different direction. Once we acknowledge our sins, freedom can soon follow. David vividly shares in Psalm 51 his struggle with God, his conscience, and his freedom after his immorality with Bathsheba. Let's look at a few select verses and see if we can make an application to our own sins:

> *Have mercy on me, O God, according to your steadfast love; according to your abundant mercy blot out my transgressions. Wash me thoroughly from my iniquity, and cleanse me from my sin! For I know my transgressions, and my sin is ever before me. Against you, you only, have I sinned and done what is evil in your sight, so that you may be justified in your words and blameless in your judgment. (Psalm 51:1–4)*

It is true that others were hurt, even murdered, by David's actions, but David is primarily focusing on his damaged relationship with

God because of this sinful act. He begins with the solution of asking for God's mercy to cleanse him from his sin. Every sin causes damage to our relationship with God and we would be wise to follow David's example. We must fall before the throne of grace and mercy to receive help when we are in need.

In Psalm 32:1–5, David expresses the same principal:

> *Blessed is the one whose transgression is forgiven, whose sin is covered. Blessed is the man against whom the LORD counts no iniquity, and in whose spirit there is no deceit. For when I kept silent, my bones wasted away through my groaning all day long. For day and night your hand was heavy upon me; my strength was dried up as by the heat of summer. I acknowledged my sin to you, and I did not cover my iniquity; I said, "I will confess my transgressions to the LORD," and you forgave the iniquity of my sin.*

Scholars tell us that this Psalm was actually written after Psalm 51, and if this were true, it would certainly explain the deep gratitude expressed by David for God's forgiveness. The point I want to focus on is that when David kept silent about his sin, he suffered greatly. I am not exactly sure what "bones wasting away" and "strength dried up as by the heat of summer" mean, but we get the picture! Nagging guilt, conviction of the Holy Spirit, and feeling that our relationship with God is lacking are always the results of unconfessed sin. Confession and repentance brought David comfort, forgiveness, and release. The same is true for us when we finally confess what God already knows.

We know in our minds that God is always with us, but we often forget that He is watching as we progress in sinful behavior. Sometimes it is helpful is to have a human, as well as God, know your struggle. Be careful whom you invite into your confidence though. The person to whom you become vulnerable must be spiritually mature enough to handle this trust. Husbands and wives need to be very careful how and what they confess to their spouses. Ideally, your spouse is the best possible person to talk to about your struggles, but that will depend on his or her maturity level and the depth of your relationship.

If you are not in a secure enough position to confess to your spouse, find a pastor, a friend (of the same gender!) or someone else whom you trust to bring into your confidence. My experience with accountability partners has been a mixed blessing over the years. I find that people who want to be set free will use the accountability freely and in the proper fashion, while if someone really does not want freedom, accountability becomes a sham relationship. Accountability helps those who want to be accountable. For example, calling a friend for prayer support when you are out of town can assist when you are tempted; however, if you want to sneak, then all the accountability programs in the world will not really assist you. Only those who desperately desire it can gain freedom.

It seems that real accountability will take place in the midst of a close, personal relationship. Spending time with someone to get to know them at a deeper level will provide some insight. If the relationship is open enough and if something changes, questions can be asked as to the cause of the change. "Why so downcast my friend? How are you doing, you look like you are struggling," etc. can all lead to freedom.

Once forgiveness is sought from God, you must then become proactive in the battle against lust and immorality. Repentance involves more than simple confession. There needs to be a change of direction! Self-control is one of the fruits of the Spirit listed in Galatians 5 and is desperately needed in our fight for purity. The scripture gives us two commands that will assist us in this fight if we follow their instruction. First:

Let us walk properly as in the daytime, not in orgies and drunkenness, not in sexual immorality and sensuality, not in quarreling and jealousy. But put on the Lord Jesus Christ, and make no provision for the flesh, to gratify its desires. (Romans 13:13–14)

We are told to walk in the daytime, meaning to stay away from activities associated with darkness—in this case, orgies, drunkenness, sexual immorality, and sensuality. Today darkness could mean attending social gatherings where alcohol and mixed company gather for the express purpose of flirting, often giving birth to immorality. "Dirty dancing" is a rage today, and I do not think it would be too much of a stretch to say that it could be considered darkness, or at least not helpful in our pursuit of purity! Paul also says to become proactive by putting on the Lord Jesus Christ and make no provision for the flesh. I am sure I do not fully understand all that means about putting Christ on, but the "no provision for my flesh" part makes perfect sense to me. As I have previously stated, I do not go to public pools or malls if I can help it. I do not venture to unknown websites, and I always check out movies with a family-oriented rating service before I watch them. My flesh does not need any help in sinning or desiring what is evil, so I attempt to starve it whenever possible. If I see something that is suggestive or sensual, I attempt to follow the law of first glance and turn away! My desires often run contrary to the Holy Spirit, and I must not make allowances or provision for their fulfillment.

While I am tap-dancing in a minefield of potentially controversial issues, let me share my experiences and feelings about dancing. I fully understand that there are other opinions and I simply offer my observations for your consideration, with no intention of making law, legalism, or a new interpretation of scripture. I mentioned "social gatherings" in the previous paragraph, and I have to wonder about the benefits of going to these types of gatherings. My experiences with bars and other such places before meeting Christ have clearly tainted my current viewpoint. The point of going dancing or to a bar in my day was to meet someone of the opposite sex in order to engage in immoral behavior. The gyrations of the female body are a constant temptation to the male eye. A gathering of many females shaking and moving to sensually oriented music is not a place where a man of God will find victory for his thought life.

I had a surreal conversation with a group of parents about swing dancing one day after church. Several young people were taking up this activity and their parents asked me my opinion of it. My experience with swing dancing was limited to movies, but what I did know was enough to offer some cautions. The parents pressed me on the issue, so I attempted to paint them a word picture. There was a woman in our church at that time who was very outgoing and relatively attractive; I will call her Sue (not her real name). I said, "What would you think if Sue and I were out swing dancing? I am grabbing Sue around the waist and swinging her between my legs and over my head. Sue is rolling across my back and then I fling her between my legs again, and so on. Would this be appropriate for us, and would it be helpful to our purity?" They admitted that it might not be the best behavior for their pastor and this woman to engage in. So I asked them, "Why do you think it is okay for your hormonally-charged teenagers to do the same?" I asked, "What about slipping as they grab for the waist or shoulders of their partner and accidentally touching their breasts or rear ends? What about swinging their partners between their legs or rolling over their backs? Is that helpful to their young lives and the struggles they are facing?" The conversation ended there and the parents walked away thinking I was overreacting. Perhaps I was, but I doubt it. I still remember the thrill and chill that went through my body the first time I touched a girl. I assume that it has not changed that much since I was young. Please, do not even get me started on Christian mosh pits!

Courage to Flee

The next command is short and sweet—Ephesians 4:27—"and give no opportunity to the devil." The word "opportunity" is often translated as place, ground, territory, or jurisdiction, all of which can be understood as military terminology. When an invasion takes place, an army attempts to set up a beachhead on the enemy's shores. The reason is so that the invaders can establish a base, bring in supplies, and make further inroads into the enemy territory. Once the beachhead has been established, the invaders can easily bring additional reinforcements and supplies ashore so the invasion can proceed. Pictures of tanks and soldiers pressing inland come to mind quite easily. What Paul was saying, I believe, is that if we give the devil an inch, he will take the proverbial mile. By allowing the enemy of our souls a place on our spiritual beach, we give him the advantage and the opportunity to take more territory. We must not allow him the beachhead in the first place!

Removing an already established enemy is no easy feat, and if you are trapped in pornography or an immoral relationship, you know what I mean. But we can and must remove him, and once we do, we must remain diligent not to allow the enemy to land on our shores again. We lost this territory little by and little, and we must retake it the same way. Each victory we achieve makes the next one a bit easier. Each time we resist the second glance, turn off the TV, shut down the computer, or walk away from an improper relationship, we become stronger. As we gain strength, the ability to resist increases and failures decrease. Sadly, the other side is true as well. Each time we give in, it becomes easier and easier to compromise repeatedly. Our hearts can become hardened or they can become softer depending on what we do with temptation. A hard heart can lead to callousness and complete deception. Every time we resist the enemy, we ensure that eventually, he will flee from us. As we gain victory over our foe, our hearts will once again become tender to the "still small voice" that we were not listening to when engaged in our sins.

One technique that I have used to assist in the battle for my thought life is implementing what are called "prayer targets." I am not sure whom to credit with this idea because I did not invent it; however, I use it almost daily! The process is fairly simple. I begin by thinking of someone who, if that person became a Christian, his or her salvation would cause great damage to the devil's kingdom. After thinking of one or more people, every time you find yourself faced with a visual or mental sexual temptation, begin to pray for that person. A young lady walks in front you with very little on, and what she is wearing is three sizes too small; begin to intercede for this young lady as well as for your prayer target. "Father, please help that young lady to understand what she is doing by dressing like that; if she is a Christian, then please open her eyes, and if she is not, then please bring her to salvation. God, would you please bring (your primary prayer target) to repentance and into your eternal kingdom. Break down any barriers that are keeping so and so from knowing You. Bring others into their lives so they can know You and be set free." Praying something like this will immediately get your mind off the young woman and put it where it belongs. It is very difficult to be absorbed in a lust-filled fantasy when you are interceding for someone else. You can pray like this as often as you like and for as long as it takes! For a person who is attempting to overcome temptation, using prayer targets works. Our enemy is no one's fool, so he will not continue to attack someone who is always turning temptations into intercessory prayer. Be aware that the battle will simply shift to another front, and as soon as you see the new attacks, pray! Prayer is the only offensive weapon listed alongside our armor in Ephesians 6. We must use it often, swinging boldly against our foe.

Fleeing, cutting it off, starving it, repenting, asking for help, making no provision for the flesh, not giving the devil an inch, and praying like crazy will all help in the battle for purity. In the next chapter, I will specifically address both men and women with some very practical advice concerning how to help one another in this pursuit of purity.

5. Yes, Cain, We Are Our Brothers' (and Sisters') Keepers!

It's their problem, not mine

Most men I know who are attempting to walk in purity hate the warm weather and sometimes secretly wished they lived at the North Pole. It is not some manly fantasy to live in a house made of ice or hunt polar bears that drives us, but a desire to escape from the "skin-fest" that begins as the weather warms up. As the temperatures rise, the clothes depart. Daily, men are faced with strapless, sleeveless, braless, backless, higher, shorter, tighter, halters, and see-throughs and all are a nightmare for the man of God attempting to win the war in his thought life. In discussing this topic with women young and old the responses vary from, "It's not my problem, all men are animals," to, "Oh, I never thought about how I dress and that it might cause someone to stumble."

Men are not complete animals; however, most men are very visually oriented. Many men become tempted when in the presence

47

of attractive women wearing sensual clothing or behaving in a seductive fashion. Words like "attractive" and "pretty" are in the eyes of the beholder, and there is no universal agreement between men as to what constitutes beauty. I speak as a man, and I realize that sometimes women cannot understand how and why men act the way they do. I cannot explain it successfully to a female any more than a woman can explain to a man the feeling of childbirth. Some things we have to take on faith, and the difference between men and women is one of those things. Why most men are drawn to certain parts of the female anatomy I cannot explain, but in discussions with my gender, most men are drawn to the female body like a moth to a flame. I am left to assume that men are attracted to the female body because God designed it that way! It is true that the women are not responsible for what the man thinks, and in that sense, those who say it is the man's problem are correct. The man of God must control his eyes and thoughts, and carefully guard what he lets his eyes settle on.

On the other hand, do the women have any responsibility for how they dress in order to prevent these visually oriented creatures from stumbling? Biblically speaking, I believe they do. Romans 14 and 15 address these issues in depth and I will not develop them here. The main idea is that we must not cause others to stumble if we can help it, and on this point, most Bible students and scholars would agree.

The word "stumble," used in scripture in this context, is not necessarily referring to tripping as much as being baited or trapped. Setting a piece of cheese on the trigger point of a mousetrap better describes the word than pushing a footstool in front of a blind person does. Men are trapped by what they see and women tend to be trapped by what they feel. We cannot help what others think or do, but we must take stock of our own words and actions. We will give an account someday to God for what we have done, and I certainly do not want to cause anyone to stumble, or to trap anyone, by my words or actions.

One time, I met with a group of teenage girls to talk specifically about modesty. In a moment of complete honesty, I asked them something like the following: "You mean to tell me that when you are getting dressed, you don't look in the mirror and say something like, 'I look sexy,' or, 'I look good, real good'?" I asked them, "You don't attempt to accent certain parts of your anatomy like your chest and rear in order to draw attention to those areas by guys?" By "real good," I mean dressing sensually in order to make guys notice them. I am not talking about being nicely dressed or putting on makeup. What I mean is dressing in a certain way to attempt to attract the attention and stares of men. Most of the girls admitted that they did such things but said they were unaware of how it *really* affected the guys. As a man, I find this hard to swallow, but I have to believe it since a group of Christian young women told me so. After I explained exactly what men looked at and why, the girls' general response was, "gross!"

Much of the current fashion draws necklines lower to expose cleavage and many times words like "sexy," "hot," and "available" are emblazoned across the chests or rear ends of those garments, the very spots where men tend to gaze. Somewhere in the secret places of her mind, a woman needs to deal with *why* she is exposing or highlighting certain parts of her body. Is it so men will whistle, or that she can get a room full of guys to turn around or to trip over chairs? Why does the fashion industry highlight chests and rear ends so much if there is ignorance as to their effects on the male crowd?

Motives need to be addressed, and women must consider what they are doing and why. If temptation *is* the goal, then the fashion industry knows it well, and Christian women need to evaluate how they dress, and what they are attempting to communicate to their brothers in the Lord. As a man, I expect this behavior from the world, but in the church of Jesus Christ, where we claim a different standard, this ought not to be done or endured. In the appendix, I have included an open letter to women in the Body of Christ that makes an appeal for women to consider what they wear to church and church functions. Please feel free to copy and distribute to any willing readers.

Men have a responsibility as well in this whole arena. I have already addressed guarding our eyes, but there is more that men must do in order to protect the women. Men can have a tremendous effect on ladies by how they talk to them, touch them, flirt with them, and look at them, so we must be careful that we are not arousing something in women that cannot be righteously fulfilled. Men who flirt are potentially creating fantasies in women, and this can lead to stumbling.

Yes, Cain, We Are Our Brother's Keepers

From what I am told, men and women both fantasize, but the pictures are very different. While men will think primarily about sexual encounters and naked bodies, the ladies are picturing a leisurely walk on the beach, or sitting next to Mr. Wonderful on the couch. Perhaps the women are picturing this man of God leading their family in devotions, or on an outreach of some type spending time with their children. Men must be careful to guard the women's emotions, and not stir up unrighteous desires.

It has amazed me, from a male point of view, to observe the type of man that a beautiful woman will run off with while deserting her family. I understand the temptation from the male point of view to chuck everything and flee with a gorgeous woman, but most of the men that women run off with are not hunks, and some are even chunks! Women are not attracted to the externals quite the way men are. It seems that, to the female sex, a lack of hair or an abundance of waistline is not nearly as important as being spiritual, sensitive, gentle, and understanding.

Men, we must pay very careful attention to flirting, inappropriate conversations, or attentiveness in our actions when dealing with women outside of our families. We do not want to steal part of a heart to which we are not entitled. Those of us who tend to be more outgoing and verbal must be aware that our words, looks, and gestures (even touching) can have the unintended consequence of causing a woman to struggle in her thought life. We must check our motives as to why we want to be the center of attention all of the time. Why do we want all the women to laugh at our jokes or to think we are Mr. Wonderful? Is it really necessary for the waitress to notice us and think we are so funny? There is nothing wrong with being friendly, but we must be careful that we are not attempting to get something beyond that with our words and actions. Would we be as comfortable with our wives surrounded by a group of laughing men as we want them to be with us in the middle of a group of women? We must examine our motives to determine if we are acting properly and righteously. Whose interest do we really have in mind? Whose should we keep first and foremost?

Men and women are responsible for their own thought lives and their behavior. However, we must be aware of how we may affect others by our dress, words, and actions. We do not want our words or actions to cause anyone to stumble, or to become ensnared in some besetting sin. We cannot carry the full burden of responsibility for what others may struggle with, but we do play a part; it is not my intention to place an undeserved load on our shoulders. However, what we should do is check our motives and see *why* we speak, act, and dress as we do. If, upon reflection, we are completely innocent and pure in our thoughts and actions, great! If not, then we need to do whatever is necessary to behave in a way that demonstrates that we are considering others as better than ourselves.

Paul leaves us little wiggle room in this passage; may we obey it:

Yes, Cain, We Are Our Brother's Keepers

Do nothing from rivalry or conceit, but in humility count others more significant than yourselves. Let each of you look not only to his own interests, but also to the interests of others. (Philippians 2:3–4)

Cain attempted to convince God that he was not responsible for Abel and God would have none of it. If we are counting others as more important, or more significant, than we are, then we will have little problem limiting our freedom for their sakes. If I know my actions are tempting someone else, and if I am attempting to obey this verse, I will not continue them. Because I value others and have an obligation to look out for them, I will limit my freedom for the sake of others. This verse applies to men in how they flirt and interact with women, and it applies to women concerning how they are dressing their "temple of the Holy Spirit." In answer to an ancient question, "Yes, Cain, we are responsible for one another, and always will be."

Let get real and practical for a moment here. Ladies, the next time you are getting dressed, ask yourself what is your clothing saying about you? What part of your body is drawing the most attention from those that would look at you? Are you wearing anything that you need to pull up because it is too low or pull down because it is too short? How about skin tight, cleavage revealing, or seductive? If you walked into a group of men what would you expect them to look at? What is your clothing saying to them? Is purity your goal or something less than that? It matters deeply so please consider these type questions when getting dressed.

Courage to Flee

Men, how do you conduct yourself around women? Are you eyeing them up and down constantly? Are you making them uncomfortable by talking to their chest? How about flirting and attempting to steal affection from them? Are you touching a woman carelessly? Have you thought about what you are saying and what they may be thinking? We must, if we love one another. We cannot simply ignore the human sexuality component in our lives.

We must think of others when we choose how to conduct our lives, and this is especially true as parents. The next chapter attempts to help parents train their children not only to survive in this sin-sick world, but also to help change it for the better.

6. Parents: Start Early, Interfere Often

Parents are older than their children for a reason

I have often said that the difference between a child that excels and avoids trouble and one that fails is one main thing—parental supervision. While this is not the only ingredient, it is a key one. Parents must know what their children are thinking and doing.

The rod and reproof give wisdom, but a child left to himself brings shame to his mother. (Proverbs 29:15)

Know well the condition of your flocks, and give attention to your herds. (Proverbs 27:23)

My wife and I used to have a small flock of goats. Well, in fact, we had two. One day I went up to the barn and saw that one of the goats had managed to become trapped in the area where we keep a hay bale for their eating pleasure. Her front leg was stuck, and she was screaming up a storm. As I helped her out, I wondered how long she had been in that twisted position. She could not help herself, and her sister certainly did not tell me. How long she was stuck I will never know, but I do know that the only way I found out was to go up to the barn!

As parents, we are given a flock to shepherd. It may be small or large, but God expects us to take care of it for Him! At least part of that responsibility is to know what the little lambs are doing, and with whom they are doing it. How do you know that your children are acting as you wish if you are not observing their behavior and conversation? How do you know that they are being kind or sharing if you cannot see or hear them? "I do not need to watch them because they are with good kids," protests the parent to me. How do you know they are good kids? Do you know how long it takes a good kid to become something less than good? While it may vary as to length of time, Proverbs state that a child left alone will eventually bring shame. How do you know if their legs are stuck somewhere they ought not to be if you do not check on them? They could be crying for hours and their brothers or sisters may not tell you. Severe damage can happen quickly, so we must be aware. Parents must check on the flocks under their care, and they must do so often.

One of the young men in my church invited me to begin using Facebook on the Internet. I agreed and ventured out into the world of cyberspace as part of my responsibility as pastor to "know well the condition of my flock." It has been both enjoyable and enlightening. I have since challenged the parents in my church to go out and visit their children's pages. Do they know who their children's friends are? Do they know what personal information is being revealed, and talked about, for the whole cyber world to see? Do they know the pictures that are out there, or the music groups their children love? If not, why not? Do the parents know who the children are texting or talking with in the multiple chat rooms that are available? Parents should know so they can assist their children to make godly decisions. Of course it takes time; shepherding is a time consuming occupation.

Parents often ask me in the midst of a crisis, "Where did I go wrong?" My response often is, "You let go too early." About the time that parents should be more involved, they are taking their hands off and giving away too much freedom to children not ready for it. We would not dream of letting our children drive our brand new cars without instruction and supervision, but we let them navigate the Internet and make potentially dangerous friendships and allow them to become emotionally and even physically involved with the opposite sex long before they are trained.

Many debate over the age when parents should let go and I will not settle the debate here. A helpful principle is that as the child demonstrates maturity and the ability to handle freedom, the parent can give more freedom. Some children are mature beyond their years and others are not; a wise parent will know the difference.

As far as I can tell, the Bible does not provide a specific age for adulthood. Eighteen and twenty-one are ages that our society has deemed as sufficient, but scripturally, there are no such arbitrary lines. I prefer to deal with the concept of being under a parent's authority rather than an age seemingly randomly selected by our secular society. Ideally, a daughter will be able to remain under her father's authority until her daddy walks her down the aisle to her waiting groom on their wedding day. The same would be true for a son, except that he is the recipient, being given the bride by another father! Some will marry younger than others, but that should be the parent's decision, and not based on some random age picked out of thin air. As a child matures and demonstrates the ability to act responsibly, more freedom can and should be given.

It is perfectly natural for girls to be attracted to boys and boys to girls and most children will enter the sexual temptation realm sooner than later. This process begins somewhat earlier with the girls, but boys catch up soon enough. As our children moved through adolescence, we had many open and honest conversations about these normal desires and drives. If the parents do not discuss such things, where will the children get their information? From the government schools? The Internet? Friends that are the same age? TV or movies? Parents are the best, and, I believe, God-chosen resource to help their children grow and understand the sexual arena.

This may be a stretch for some parents, but it is well worth the effort and discomfort you may experience to ensure that your children are well prepared to face the hormonal battle that will soon be upon them. God designed the attraction between male and female, and parents are the proper resource to explain how best to channel that attraction until it can be righteously fulfilled.

The previous chapters in this book apply to our children as well. Boys need to be careful about stirring up emotions in girls and girls need to be aware of how they dress their temple of the Holy Spirit. One of my daughters is very affectionate and loves to hug and touch people as a sign of affection. We had to explain to her that touching a young man's knee might not mean the same thing to her as it does to him, especially if he is lovesick! She needed to guard herself around young men and be aware of what she was doing in order to protect them.

This same daughter wanted to wear a miniskirt. We asked her *why* she wanted to wear one and her reply was interesting. "The guys are all attracted to the girls that show more skin and I want them to like me, too," was her explanation. We could not deny the fact that the young men did follow the young ladies around who were dressed in that way, but we encouraged our daughter to check her heart motives. "Is that really the type of man you want to marry? Do you want to chuck your values simply to get some guy to goggle over you?" Many such questions were asked and multiple conversations followed. She eventually saw our logic and agreed that it was more important to please God and her parents than some young man that she most likely would not end up marrying. For the record, I would not have allowed her to wear the skirt outside of her bedroom anyway, but I was more concerned about her motives than the clothing.

Underneath our choices rest multiple motives and we must understand and deal with these motives. Simply putting a bunch of rules in place without understanding motives can lead to legalism.

In my opinion, many parents allow their children to become involved with the opposite sex excessively early. Relationships can become very passionate and emotionally binding at a young age, while, realistically, neither party is ready or able to marry.

We attempted to acknowledge the attraction that our children may have developed toward someone, acknowledging that it was part of the normal developmental process, and then began to discuss what to do with it. When children are pre-teen or early- to mid-teen, they cannot marry, and encouraging them in relationships with someone is setting them up for heartache and potential disaster.

Parents need to be aware of what their sons or daughters are thinking, and with whom they are involved, even if only in their minds. Children need their parents to help them process the confusing emotions that they will inevitably face.

We attempted to avoid the sexual problems associated with traditional dating by encouraging our children to wait until they were old enough to consider marriage before becoming involved in relationships. Dating and going steady often prepare someone better for divorce than for a life-long marital commitment. I believe it is wiser to wait until it can be righteously fulfilled before awakening love and sexual desire in our young people.

As a pastor, I do a significant amount of pre-marriage counseling and most young couples struggle with sexual desire for their soon-to-be spouses. This is natural and increases as the honeymoon approaches. The young people who have drawn clear lines on physical touching, and have practiced parental inclusion, are usually successful in avoiding moral failure. The ones who do not protect themselves through parental involvement, and do not have clear lines drawn regarding physical contact, usually fail.

What are your children watching in their rooms or listening to on those headphones? Who is your child e-mailing or texting? When they go out at night, do you know where they are going, and with whom they are spending time? Do you have access to your child's e-mail account or cell phone records? Do you know what websites your child has visited lately? Some may call this snooping; I call it being involved. If your child is resistant to your knowing, shouldn't that bother you? What is there to hide anyway?

Typically, things done under the cover of darkness and secrecy bring death and destruction. If your child is viewing pornography already, wouldn't it be better to help him or her get over it now, instead of waiting until it is an addiction? Parents must be involved and active in order to assist their children in developing the necessary skills to survive in this lust-crazed world. The training must begin when children are young and be consistently applied as long as they are under their parents' roofs.

Even with patient, consistent instruction, children can still make foolish choices; after they have grown up and left your home, however, they would be choosing against what they know, instead of simply making an uninformed choice. We must give our children a fighting chance to make it in this world, and it begins almost from the day they are born!

"Well, I agree with some of what you just wrote, but it sounds like it will take a lot of time," you may be thinking. You are absolutely correct! Talking, the willingness to interfere, confrontation, the challenging of incorrect assumptions, and what I call "intense fellowship" are all parts of an involved parent's tasks. No one ever said that parenting was easy. To be effective, it involves a great deal of self-sacrifice and time on the parent's part.

The training of their children has been delegated to parents from the very hand of God, and we must be willing to invest ourselves completely in the task (See Deuteronomy 6). In the scripture, children are referred to as "gifts" and "fruit," and we must take care of them with all diligence. Investing time in our children will not guarantee that they will never fail, but if they do fall, it will not be because we did not attempt to train them. Our efforts can help them get ready for the world they will face as they leave our home. We must prepare them. If we do not, who will?

Parents need to help their children understand from a young age what lust is and how to defeat it. We need to teach our sons the law of first glance, and train our daughters the proper way to handle their bodies around men. We need to instruct them about the proper role of sex inside of marriage, and not let them be trained by Hollywood or the Internet.

As our children move into puberty, parents should be the ones discussing what is occurring in them physically, emotionally, and spiritually. The task should not be left to some perverted producer of pornography or some other humanistic purveyor. Our sons will be exposed to an almost constant barrage of sensuality; are they ready? Will our daughters be part of the problem, or will they be part of a group that helps raise up a new standard of modesty and decency?

I sometimes marvel at fathers and husbands and wonder if they have forgotten what it is like to be male. Perhaps it is more complicated than that; maybe they are fearful of confrontation, but allowing their wives or daughters to dress sensually is foolish at best, and opening the door for immorality at worst.

I wonder why some men do not look at their wives or daughters and place themselves in the mindset of other men. Do you really want other men's eyes drawn to your wives' or daughters' cleavage, or skintight clothes highlighting their chests or rear ends? Are you secretly proud of how they look, perhaps wanting to show them off, and encouraging them to wear clothing that is excessively tight? If that is true, or even partially true, what kind of motive is that? Have you forgotten the struggles that you have with someone else's wife or daughter? Perhaps it would be beneficial to take another look at what we allow or encourage and recheck our motives. Is purity our goal, or sensuality or pride? Are we comparing our styles and actions to the world's system or to God's Word? Are we adding to the degradation of our culture or attempting to present a higher standard? Only you can answer these questions for yourself, but your family desperately needs you to do it! The church needs you to do it, and our society needs you to take a second look and make sure holiness and modesty are the goals.

Changes come slowly, but perhaps they would take place more quickly if each family addressed these issues in addition to the organized church. If we addressed these issues at home, we would present a very clear difference to the world around us. Based on what is currently popular within the church world, there is very little difference between the Christian and the world.

I hear men and women of God both young and old saying to and about each other, "You look hot!" or, "That is such a hot dress." I wonder if the people who are saying such things are actually aware of what they sound like. Is the goal of a godly woman to be "hot"? What does that mean anyway?

In my BC days (Before Christ), we used a numbering system of sorts, with ten being the best looking, and one being on the other end of the scale. What were we evaluating? The scale was really a lust meter and Christians have adopted it! When a husband tells his wife that she looks "hot" in the privacy of their home, that is one thing, but does he really want other men looking at what he alone is allowed to enjoy? The same would hold true with our daughters. Have we adopted the world's system of lust and embraced it so much that we do not even think about it anymore? Is there any connection between these issues and the skyrocketing divorce rate of Christians? What do we stir up in our wives if we encourage them to be seductive? What will happen if a wife is "hot" and ends up running off with some other man who enjoyed her "hotness"? Will we then be glad that we promoted this philosophy? What about the well-documented fact that the vast majority of young people cast off their parents' faith, and many end up in immorality, shortly after they leave the home? Are there any connections? We must find the answer as parents if the church and family are to survive. We must be willing to go before the throne of the King and ask His opinion of such matters.

I already know some of God's views on such topics. Carefully consider the following verses and think about what our sensual world system promotes, and if we as believers in Jesus Christ should imitate that philosophy:

Do not be conformed to this world, but be transformed by the renewal of your mind, that by testing you may discern what is the will of God, what is good and acceptable and perfect. (Romans 12:2)

Now we have received not the spirit of the world, but the Spirit who is from God, that we might understand the things freely given us by God. (I Corinthians 2:12)

You adulterous people! Do you not know that friendship with the world is enmity with God? Therefore whoever wishes to be a friend of the world makes himself an enemy of God. (James 4:4)

Do not love the world or the things in the world. If anyone loves the world, the love of the Father is not in him. For all that is in the world— the desires of the flesh and the desires of the eyes and pride in possessions—is not from the Father but is from the world. (1 John 2:15–16)

Beloved, do not imitate evil but imitate good. Whoever does good is from God; whoever does evil has not seen God. (3 John 1:11)

We need to evaluate seriously our standards and desires in light of these verses. The world system stands in direct opposition to the Kingdom of God, and we must be careful not to imitate our enemy. We must train our children to recognize the world system and how it wants to dilute the Christian message. We can only serve one Lord, and it must be Jesus!

We as parents must be involved with the lives of our children and help them navigate in the sexual realm. If you have been on the sidelines, it is time to get involved. If you have not been involved, start now. Have a family meeting and share what you think. Explain why you want to change directions, and begin today. If your children are grown share with them what you have seen and pray that the Lord will touch their hearts as they train your grandchildren.

Many have fallen into bondage and more will join them in our lifetime. Maybe you are one of them. One passage that constantly gives me hope is:

At one time we too were foolish, disobedient, deceived and enslaved by all kinds of passions and pleasures. We lived in malice and envy, being hated and hating one another. (Titus 3:3)

The "at one time" means they were no longer living for those things and the same should be true for all believers. We used to live in bondage but now we are free. In the appendix there is an article entitled *The Formerly's* that might provide some encouragement, as will the next chapter.

7. Is There Hope for Those Who Have Failed?

We all fall, but let's get back up and not sleep there

n Christ there is always hope! Proverbs 24:16 states, "for the righteous falls seven times and rises again, but the wicked stumble in times of calamity." My prayer has always been that when I fall, I fall in the right direction, and on the right path. I know I will fail, but I desire to fall towards the Lord, and whilst I am traveling on the Highway of Holiness (Isaiah 35:8). Each time I fail, I can learn something of value, and therefore the experience is not wasted. Several verses give me hope about the process. This will not be an in-depth theological analysis of these verses, but I trust they will offer some encouragement to those who struggle.

And we all, with unveiled face, beholding the glory of the Lord, are being transformed into the same image from one degree of glory to another. For this comes from the Lord who is the Spirit. (2 Corinthians 3:18)

For me the difficulty rests in that little word "to," which falls between the glories. I love to be in the glory and I cannot wait until the next glory; it is that process in between that causes all the problems! By "glory," I mean being pure, in a great relationship with God, growing spiritually, being at peace and rest, etc. Through the Spirit, the Lord transforms us *into* something that we currently are not. The process involves trials, disappointments, and temptations. As we mature, we fail less, grow more, and begin to look different than we did when we began our journey. As an old saying goes, "If you fail, it does not mean you are a failure." Therefore, there is hope in Christ that we are being changed; God even uses our failures to mold us into what He desires. I am not the same man I was twenty or thirty years ago, and I will not be the same ten years in the future as I am today. God is at work! We enjoy the glory while in it, and endure the "to" until the next glory arrives.

> *And I am sure of this, that he who began a good work in you will bring it to completion at the day of Jesus Christ. (Philippians 1:6)*

Paul was assuring the young believers in Philippi that God was able to do as He promised. God began a good work in us when we became His children, and He is more than able to complete the task in spite of our failures. The process begins after salvation, and it is finished upon our deaths when finally we step into Life. We spend our lives on this side of eternity in growth and change as we walk out the "good work" that was begun in us by our Lord. Jesus began the work and He is faithful to His word to complete it. We must not give into despair.

> *For we are his workmanship, created in Christ Jesus for good works,*
> *which God prepared beforehand, that we should walk in them.*
> *(Ephesians 2:10)*

No matter how we may feel, or whatever falsehoods our enemy whispers into our ears, we are masterpieces in progress! God does not make junk, and whatever He touches ends up being wonderful. We are *His* workmanship, and God will do whatever is necessary to complete *His* work to *His* satisfaction. Even if we are trapped in sin, bound by the enemy, or ensnared by our own foolish choices, God is able to free us, and He will do whatever is necessary to bring us to a finished work.

The word workmanship can be translated as masterpiece. We often do not feel like anything special because we are aware of all of our failures, but God sees us as perfect, complete, hand-crafted masterpieces! If God is working on us, we will end up just fine when He is finished. God cannot fail and He will not regarding us.

There are many other verses to consider, but these three will serve as a foundation to give us hope. Even if we have failed, God is bigger than our failures, and He is able to redeem, restore, and make us new. Of course, there are consequences to our actions, and we play a part in the process by our obedience, but "hopeless" and "God" cannot exist in the same sentence! Three of the greatest words repeatedly found in the scripture are, "God is able." Our sins are not bigger or stronger than our God is. Our addictions are no match compared to His power to provide release and freedom. God challenged Israel through Isaiah's words in Isaiah 1:18:

> *Come now, let us reason together, says the LORD: though your sins are like scarlet, they shall be as white as snow; though they are red like crimson, they shall become like wool.*

Whatever your sin, and however far you may have fallen, you cannot descend to a place beyond God's reach. Someone will always bring up "the unpardonable sin" at this point. If you are reading this, and you are concerned that you have committed the unpardonable sin, that is most likely proof that you have not! While theologians argue over what that sin actually is, most would agree that if you had committed it, you would not care that you had.

For sins other than the unknown, unpardonable one, we need to remember what John the Beloved states:

> *1 John 1:9: "If we confess our sins, he is faithful and just to forgive us our sins and to cleanse us from all unrighteousness."*

This is a faithful promise from the only One that can forgive sins - if we confess, He will forgive. Not only will He forgive and cleanse us, but He will restore us back to fellowship with Him.

Is There Hope For Those Who Have Failed?

What role do other believers play in the process of redemption? The scripture gives clear direction on the topic of how to deal with sin and failures in each other.

> *Brothers, if anyone is caught in any transgression, you who are spiritual should restore him in a spirit of gentleness. Keep watch on yourself, lest you too be tempted. (Galatians 6:1)*

When someone confesses his or her sins to us, we must take this verse to heart. This verse actually speaks about being caught, discovered, or trapped in sin, and not just freely confessing it, but the principle is the same. We must restore those captured by sin and take care that we as well are not carried away by it. Restoring means that the sinner is welcomed back into fellowship with no strings attached. The restored brother or sister is not relegated to a second class citizen, but they are viewed through the blood of Jesus Christ.

I am not saying that trust is given immediately, for often that takes time to rebuild, but immediate forgiveness and restoration of fellowship is commanded as soon as the sin is confessed. We need to use wisdom in the process of restoration, of course, but withholding love and forgiveness is not an option. For example, if someone struggles with stealing, placing him or her in a position dealing with money is unwise. In our context, if a man has a problem with lust, then allowing him to head up a women's aerobics class, or be a leader to girls or women in any fashion, is placing him at risk of failing again.

The organized church also can and must play a role in helping its members fight this onslaught of sensuality. Counseling can be provided for those who are trapped in the grips of pornography. Marriage counseling should be provided to assist couples that are struggling, remembering to place safeguards up to prevent affairs between the counselors and counselees. There can be men's and women's support groups to provide a place for open discussion and prayer. Accountability practices can be discussed and organized. Teaching on the topics of modesty, relational integrity, and holiness should regularly take place from the pulpit. Classes training parents on how to help prepare their children should be offered. We must help parents train their children, from a young age, to be aware of the subtle draw of sensuality, and help them prepare to survive in a sex-saturated society.

Church leaders must be role models, demonstrating how to survive in this sexually saturated culture, and should provide a proven track record of success. Older men and women must invest in younger ones, sharing with them their victories and defeats. Each generation does not need to reinvent the wheel and repeat the same mistakes. The older generation should transfer its wisdom to the younger, and the church should provide a vehicle to help make this happen. This is not an all-inclusive list, but our churches would be significantly strengthened if just these few suggestions were implemented. The church must be willing to address the issues openly and firmly from a biblical viewpoint, and to challenge society's never-ending messages of lust and sensuality.

Leaders must help those who are still trapped and go after the wandering sheep. Pastors must become proactive if we hope to turn back this tidal wave of immorality! The church should encourage its members to examine their motives and desires by comparing them to the Word of God, as opposed to this world's system. These are a just a few suggestions that the church could implement to help the struggling saints! As leaders, we must seek God for wisdom, knowing that He will provide creative ideas to help train and heal His people in this battle for moral purity.

God uses the most unlikely people to accomplish His work. Past failure does not disqualify you. In fact, your failure might provide the perfect opportunity to assist someone else to avoid the same mistakes and heartaches that you endured. The apostle Paul was a persecutor of the church and Peter denied the Lord, yet both were used mightily by God. David committed murder and adultery, yet he remained "a man after God's own heart." The key was their repentance and the ability to receive forgiveness and grace from God. If you have failed, go to the One that can redeem you and restore you. God is still using donkeys. I should know; I am one! I was once a drugged-laced rebel who simply lived for the next high and immoral relationship. Now, by God's redeeming grace, I am a born-again, saved masterpiece in progress! You also can be a masterpiece in progress if you will cry out to God for help, forgiveness, and purpose.

If you have fallen, or if you are a recovering "formerly," how do you keep from being ensnared again, or ending right back in the mess of pornography or immorality? Perhaps you have not fallen, but are now more aware of the potential to do so. How do you stay on the highway of holiness? "We must be on our guard, for our enemy prowls around like a lion looking for someone to devour" (1 Peter 5:8). I have heard some state that the devil is a toothless lion. If that is true, then he has gummed many to death! How do we not end up as lion's food? The next chapter will address the answers.

8. Be On Your Guard—Always!

Beware of the sucker punch

Chinese proverb states, "A journey of a thousand miles begins with a single step." The easiest way to avoid adultery, pornography addiction, becoming trapped in lust, or being involved in an immoral or improper relationship is never to take the first step! If we do not make any room in our lives for these issues, they will not be able to take up residence in our heart and minds in the first place. The simple young man mentioned in Proverbs 7, would not have ended up in the house of the dead if he would have never passed by the seductress' street corner.

I am not saying that we cannot be tempted, for that is impossible. Jesus was tempted, but He did not sin. We will be tempted with all of the issues that we are discussing, and we want to be prepared and prudent, not unwise and foolish. We want to help prepare our sons and daughters for the battles that await them in our world. Forgive my use of clichés, but "an ounce of prevention is worth a pound of cure."

Drawing lines that we will not cross before being faced with the temptation is far wiser than attempting to make a choice in the heat of the moment. Even strong standards and clear lines drawn are no guarantee that we will not fail, but if we do not prepare, we will certainly fail. Although parking an ambulance at the foot of a cliff will help in healing the broken and hurting, it is wiser to put up barricades at the top to keep people from going over in the first place!

So, what can we do to help in this battle with lust and sensuality? First, we need to make sure that our hearts are in the right relationship with God. We need to be feeding our souls with the Word of God daily and continuing to grow in our awareness of the Spirit's presence in our lives. If we only eat once a week at the church service, we are anemic. If we only worship once a week, again we will be too weak to resist the battle. We need to be meeting daily with our Supreme Commander to get our strength and orders.

When the disciples of Jesus were beginning to grasp that He was leaving them, He made an incredible statement, which I am sure they had a hard time believing:

> *Nevertheless, I tell you the truth: it is to your advantage that I go away, for if I do not go away, the Helper will not come to you. But if I go, I will send him to you. (John 16:7)*

Jesus told the truth, the Holy Spirit did come upon the disciples, and they were changed men. From cowards hiding in an upper room, they were changed into mighty warriors for Christ and His Gospel; the book of Acts records this transformation. We also have the Holy Spirit in our lives to teach us, comfort us, convict us, enable us, and lead us in the paths of righteousness. We must learn to hear His voice and become intimate with the Word of God through the indwelling presence of the Holy Spirit.

The greatest danger Christians face is not a direct assault from Satan, but a drifting from their relationship with God. When we let our time of prayer, Bible study, and fellowship with other believers wane, we are an easy target of the devil. If we are having regular times of prayer and study of God's Word, keeping His Word as our standard, we are not as easily deceived, and our guard remains high; our discernment is more active. We then become more difficult targets to hit and to take out!

While I was snorkeling in the Philippines on a short-term mission's trip, the reality of drifting became vividly clear to me. I was not a very good swimmer, so I stayed in the shallows enjoying the extremely clear water. However, my head was down, and I did not pay attention to where I was in reference to the shoreline. The fish were spectacular, and the coral amazing, so I simply kept looking, and looking, and looking. What I did not realize was how far out I had drifted. In a short period of time, I was way too far out to sea for a swimmer of my skill level, and when I looked up; my prayer life was greatly enhanced! It really does not take too much for a believer to drift into dangerous territory. If we ignore our time with God for a day, the next day becomes easier to forget. Soon, a few days turn into a week, then a month. Before long, we have lost our intimacy and we feel disconnected from God and wonder why.

Just as drifting is extremely dangerous, swimming alone is also very hazardous. I heard a man give the following illustration and it really made an impression on me: "Bricks that are cemented into a wall are much harder to carry off than the ones sitting off by themselves," he said. Then, he attempted to dig a brick out of the middle of a wall and it was nearly impossible. However, he had a pile of bricks nearby and he walked over and simply picked one up and left without any effort. The visual had a very powerful effect on me. We need other believers to help "cement" us in the Body of Christ. The connections made by maintaining fellowship with other Christians are very important to our spiritual survival. These relationships help provide a level of protection and accountability that are unavailable to the loner.

Giving our hearts and lives to God is the most personal decision we will ever make, but once we have done so, we will never be alone again! We become part of a huge family, and our relationships help to hold us in place, just as the cement holds the bricks in a wall. I have often observed that when people abandon fellowship, they tend to drift and become easy prey to our enemy. We all need people in our lives who are close enough to us to challenge us and correct us as needed. "The wounds of a friend are better than the kisses of an enemy" (Proverbs 27:6). We need people who are not afraid to challenge our behavior when we are drifting off. We need to have close enough relationships that our friends and family can detect a change in our spiritual and emotional condition.

An early signal of trouble brewing is when we begin to cut off relationships that are convicting. Sin loves the darkness and hates being around the light. Comments like, "I feel judged when I am around them," begin to creep into our thoughts. The truth may be that our own actions have changed, and we now feel uncomfortable around the people who used to be friends. We really do not want to hear their viewpoints or comments about our behavior, so we avoid them, and, even blame them for "looking down on us" or "thinking poorly of us." If asked, the people are probably just very concerned about decisions we are making and are not thinking badly at all about us. We are the ones who have changed, not them. When we drift, God does not move, and if we want to get back to where we were, we must move back towards Him.

As we are daily being filled with the Spirit, and having our minds renewed in the Word of God, we then can take some reasonable precautions to provide a layer of protection against this area of lust and sensuality. Remember the law of first glance; practice it religiously! Turn your eyes away from the temptation. I sometimes joke about having sunburn on my throat as I look upwards so often to avoid what is in front of me. Walk out of the movie, turn off the TV, and close down the Internet. Remember, addictions begin with an initial step. Refuse to take that first step, and you will not end up defeated. Starvation is the only sure cure to any addiction, including sexual ones. Check the contents of movies and videos before you watch them. Multiple websites and books are readily available to assist in evaluating *before* you rent it or go to see it (see appendix). It is far better never to have the images in your mind than to have to battle them the rest of your life. It is amazing to me that I have a hard time remembering what I did yesterday, but images from my teen years are as vibrant today as they were back then. Maintaining a clean mind is so much easier than attempting to get back to one after being exposed to sinful images.

If you have a computer, make sure that anyone walking by can easily see the screen. Put the computer in the center of the room if necessary! Sin loves to hide in darkness, and one of the cures is to turn up the light! Be very careful about allowing your children unsupervised access to the World Wide Web. Make sure you know what they are doing, and what they are viewing. Install parental controls and monitoring systems. If you are already trapped in Internet pornography, take a fast from the computer for a month or more. Then slowly reintroduce the computer back into your life with strict guidelines and accountability. This is war, and your soul hangs in the balance of your choices. Do whatever is necessary to win! This is not the time for compromise or laziness. If you genuinely want freedom, it is available. It will cost you time, effort, energy, and humility, but the freedom is worth it!

When I maintained an office at a church building, I established some very rigid personal rules. Several mocked me for taking such precautions until the senior pastor left town with another woman; then, amazingly, I looked very wise! Some of my rules included that I would not meet alone with a woman in my office without the door being open, and I wanted to have a window in my office door. If possible, I would not drive alone with my secretary (or any other woman), anywhere, ever. I would not hold hands to pray with a woman outside of my family if possible. I would not counsel a woman alone, and would limit my phone counseling to two sessions. To this day, I try not to talk with the opposite sex about personal family problems or issues, for these are potential breeding grounds for bonding.

You can also have your spouse meet and talk to your co-workers to provide insight that you may have missed. It is interesting what a woman can tell about another woman, and the same is true with men. I can usually tell if a man has clear eyes, and if he would be someone that I would want around my wife or daughters. My wife has warned me occasionally to be careful about another woman, and I have heeded her advice! As a man attempting to walk in moral purity, I need all the help I can get! Most women can discern if their husbands need to be careful around someone, while many times the husband is oblivious to the danger. The same is true for the wife. Better to be safe, and err on being too careful, than to live a life of regret.

I have never regretted taking precautions, but I am sure I would be sorry if I had not. The pain, heartache, and destruction caused by not being careful far outweigh any inconvenience caused by being cautious. I have refused to meet women alone for counseling, and received their criticism, but I would gladly endure their wrath rather than to fall in sexual sin. I told them that I would be more than willing to meet them with someone else present, preferably their husbands, but they were unwilling, and, therefore, so was I. I still do not regret it. I heard Charles Swindoll on the radio quoting a study regarding pastors. Out of every twenty men that enter the ministry, only one will stay until he retires. I want to finish strong, and I am willing to endure whatever criticism is necessary to avoid falling sexually.

Since I started my own church, I have kept my office at home. We have a lovely building with a very nice office in it that is spacious and even includes a fireplace, yet I still have my office at home. My wife is usually around, and there is a measure of protection from sexual temptation in this choice. My reason for having a home office is simple. I do not want to deal with the problem of meeting women alone at my office. A friend of mine lost his ministry because he did not take these types of precautions. The pastor had his office in his church building, and was often alone. One day a woman came in crying and pretended to need counseling. As he began to talk to her, she undressed and seduced him right in his office. I do not need that temptation or opportunity to fail, so I stay home!

In addition, if you office by yourself you are vulnerable to accusation; in our current prejudiced environment against Christianity, that is all it takes to destroy your ministry. An accusation of impropriety will destroy your work. Even if your church survives, those that stay with you will be tainted by the "he said, she said" battle. The Bible speaks wisdom in 1 Thessalonians 5:22: "Abstain from all appearance of evil." I do not want to give anyone the opportunity to accuse me of anything dishonorable. I make enough mistakes as it is!

As men, we also need to be careful how we talk to all women, and make sure we are acting in purity. Paul the mentor instructed younger Timothy on how to deal with people properly:

> *Do not rebuke an older man but encourage him as you would a father, younger men as brothers, older women as mothers, younger women as sisters, in all purity. (I Timothy 5:1–2)*

This verse in our context means we as men must be careful to protect and guard a woman's heart and emotions. Flirtatious, sensual talk or improper conversations should always be off limits. Unless the woman is your wife or daughter, it is probably not proper to be providing protection emotionally, or even to provide a listening ear to her emotional difficulties. By simply listening, you may be causing the woman to stumble by providing an opportunity for emotional entanglement. I understand that there are counseling situations, but again, you must be very careful to make sure you are not bonding with someone other than your spouse. Emotional attraction can easily lead to physical relationships, and Paul's words ring loudly in my ear—flee!

I like the New American Standard translation of 1 Corinthians 7:1:

"Now concerning the things about which you wrote, it is good for a man not to touch a woman."

Placing your hands on a woman's shoulders or around her waist is not helpful. You need to be very careful not to arouse desire by how or where you touch someone other than your spouse. You do not know what struggles others may be facing, so you need to err on the side of caution. Some think I am weird, but I do not give frontal hugs to women if I can help it, but only side ones. I do not need to feel a woman's breasts in my chest, and she does not need my arms around her! Maybe I *am* weird, but I am attempting to maintain a pure thought life, and desperate times demand desperate measures!

As mentioned in an earlier chapter, I avoid, as one friend of mine likes to say, "target-rich environments." Apparently, in the military, this statement is used when a sniper or shooter has several targets in his or her line of sight, and can make the choice of which one to take out. Concerning this discussion, I am not talking about literally shooting anyone, but I am talking about staying away from situations where there a significant number of visual temptations! Hanging around dance or exercise groups of women in spandex is not helpful to me. The same can be said about swimming pools, where there is typically an abundance of skin and cleavage. If we are serious about maintaining or achieving freedom from lust, we will have to change our viewing behavior.

Planning can also help prevent failure. If you know that on your drive to work or way to the grocery store, there is a suggestive billboard that is impossible to ignore, change your driving route. Avoid the grocery store check out lines if you cannot look away from the magazines. If you have to travel and the TV is an issue, ask the motel to disconnect it, or if they will not, unplug it as soon as you enter the room. This is war, and we must be diligent if we hope to achieve victory. When we finally hate our sin as much as we once loved it, we will do whatever is necessary to get free from it. I pray we arrive at this point before we lose everything that is dear to us.

For the women reading this, there are multiple things that you can do to help the men, as well as to guard your hearts from lust and emotional entanglement. For example, stay under the protection of your husband if you are married or under your father if you are not. Make sure that your heart is totally given to the Lord first, then to your husband or father after that. If your marriage is not what you dreamed it would be, then evaluate *your* behavior, and see what *you* can change. The temptation is presented that you would be happier if you were married to someone else, but that is an illusion. Happiness comes from within, not from your circumstances. If you are a married woman, your desire must be for your husband and not for any other man. Fantasizing about TV or movie characters, or any other man, is not helpful and will produce frustration as you compare these myths to your reality. Reading endless romance novels or love stories will not help your thought life, either, and will rob you of contentment. Remember, these stories are called fiction for a reason!

The truth is that other men have multiple issues and problems just as your husband does. If you feel like you are being drawn to another man, flee.

Communication is typically the doorway to problems, so shut off all talking in the chat room, or break off the e-mail communication, for nothing of spiritual value will follow. Stop the emotional entanglement before it blossoms into a full-blown problem. Starvation is the key for you, just as it is for the man. Cut off the relationship and be brutal about it if you hope to survive. Do not make any room for another man in your heart or life.

Watch your heart regarding flirtations with men. I know most women want to be appreciated for their appearance, but this desire can only righteously be fulfilled within the context of marriage. Dressing or acting in a way to gain attention from a man or men other than your husband is not proper. Why do we do the things we do? We must ask.

With the proliferation of social media, we must learn to take our thoughts captive in even more ways. Old boyfriends and girlfriends can now find us in any number of ways through the internet. Is it really going to help you in our walk with the Lord to reconnect with your old high school flame via FaceBook? I doubt it. In fact, many marriages are now destroyed by just such connections. Be careful. Use wisdom and check your heart motives. If you find that you are hiding a social media connection from your spouse, you probably should cut if off. Now. Right now.

If you need to talk to someone and you cannot discuss such matters with your husband, then seek out a godly older woman for guidance. (See Titus 2:3-4) Pouring out your problems to another man will not help either of you. As you talk to a man, he will respond to you by wanting to protect you, and he will be tempted to cross some lines that he should not. You will end up being tempted to find security in him, instead of in the Lord and your husband. Do not go down that path, for the end is destruction. Do whatever is necessary to cut this emotional bonding off before it takes root, and you will save the needless heartache of attempting to break it after it has taken hold.

If you are unmarried then find your joy in serving others. If God wants you to be married, He is more than able to provide a spouse for you in the proper timing. "Seek God first and His kingdom and all these other things will be added unto you" (Matthew 6:33). Looking for meaning and happiness in an earthly relationship is like grasping smoke. People can never take the place of God, and attempting to place them there will only lead to frustration and disappointment.

I challenged my middle daughter to invest in the lives of others as she waited for Mr. Right. Her older sister and younger brother were both married, and she was counting the years as she waited. As she passed twenty-five, twenty-six, twenty-seven, the pressure was immense. "What's wrong with me?" she would ask. My answer was always the same, "God is able." I would also say, "It is far better to be happily married for forty years than miserably married for fifty, and if you have to wait ten years, it is worth it!" At twenty-eight, she did marry and it was well worth the wait! During her wedding, thirty or forty young girls in whom she had invested sang in a choir, and it was a wonderful testimony of years well spent waiting for her Prince Charming. Those little girls will never forget the investment made in their lives by this older girl.

True satisfaction is found in investing in others, never in selfishness. Paul presents instructions for singles clearly in 1 Corinthians 7, especially in verses 32–34:

> *I want you to be free from anxieties. The unmarried man is anxious about the things of the Lord, how to please the Lord. But the married man is anxious about worldly things, how to please his wife, and his interests are divided. And the unmarried or betrothed woman is anxious about the things of the Lord, how to be holy in body and spirit. But the married woman is anxious about worldly things, how to please her husband.*

Being single is an opportunity to serve the Lord without distraction, and it is a waste to squander those years in frustration over not being married. If God does bring a potential mate into your life, make sure that you both love the Lord with all your heart, and that seeking His kingdom is priority number one. If you begin a relationship, keep the marriage bed pure and set up some strong guidelines for your physical relationship. Touching and kissing will lead to petting and increase your sexual struggles. We challenged our children to limit the touching and keep the sexual drive in check until the honeymoon. The physical relationship is very pleasurable, and following the God-given guidelines will protect and enhance the experience. Sadly, the opposite is true as well. Tasting the sexual delights of marriage before you say "I do" causes many problems that will hinder the marriage for its duration. Many counseling problems in marriage can be easily traced back to premarital sexual experimentation. Guilt and mistrust are unleashed between the couple, and the seeds of destruction for the marriage are planted before it even begins. Typically, the wife will feel used by her husband and not protected by the premarital sexual failure. She struggles with questions like, "Why was it wrong to do this before the wedding night, but now it is okay?" In addition, she will be tempted to feel like the sexual act is dirty or dark. It is far better to wait until the honeymoon and then let sexual love be fulfilled.

Lust is never satisfied, and selfish love only seeks its own fulfillment. If one of the partners is driven by either of these, strongly consider postponing the wedding or breaking up for a season. Several pastors I know rigidly enforce a six-month postponement of the wedding if the couple fails sexually. This allows the couple to make sure that they are getting married for the right reasons, and that lust is not the foundation on which they are attempting to build.

Following God's way will bring joy and harmony; the other, bitterness and destruction. Set up some guidelines and hold to them for the sake of your future relationship! Limit touching and avoid kissing, for this usually leads to more desires that cannot be righteously fulfilled. If the temptation is too strong, make a commitment never to place yourselves in a situation where you will be alone. "We cannot understand why we keep falling into sexual sin," stated one couple. Upon examination, I discovered that they continued to ride alone at night in the car; they kept pulling off the road into some dark out-of-way place and getting into the back seat. Failure is certainly guaranteed with that type of behavior! Now, if they had brought along someone else, the temptation would have had no way to be fulfilled, and thus could have been easily avoided. Strict guidelines agreed upon before the sexual temperature has risen will help cool things off! Once the passions start flowing, the mind becomes very creative in rationalization, and failure will follow. Make your preparations before you face temptation, and success can be enjoyed.

The battle rages for purity, and we must engage and defeat the enemy! Draw some clear lines and take a stand. If you have failed, get back up and reenter the fray. We must resist our foe so he will flee. You can be free and you can avoid failing by making wise choices and avoiding tempting situations.

In the next chapter, I want to look at what we could possibly do with our freedom. We live our lives in community and part of job here on earth is to assist others.

9. The Goal of Freedom

You mean it's not all about me?

After we achieve a measure of freedom in our lives, it is not time to relax, but to expand the battle into the enemy's territory. If we look around us, it will not be too big a challenge to find someone who needs help, and God will typically bring the exact people that *you* can help into your path. Consider this passage:

> *Blessed be the God and Father of our Lord Jesus Christ, the Father of mercies and God of all comfort, who comforts us in all our affliction, so that we may be able to comfort those who are in any affliction, with the comfort with which we ourselves are comforted by God. (2 Corinthians 1:3–4)*

When pressed by someone as to why something bad happened to them, I often fall back on this section of scripture as a *possible* reason. God, of course, knows the full purpose, but He gives us a glimpse of

93

how His kingdom works in these verses. We receive comfort from God as we walk through trials and difficulties. After we have passed the trials, we are then able to comfort others with what we have learned, and share with them the help that we were given by God.

After you become battle-tested in the arena of sexual purity, God will often bring other people into your life that you can help! Someone passed the concept of "prayer targets" on to me, and now I use them. I am passing them on to everyone who reads this and perhaps they will be helpful. The "law of second glance" is not something I made up, but it is a tool I use almost daily. If you follow the law, and it works for you, perhaps you can pass it on to assist some other person in the struggle to keep his or her mind pure. Everything contained in this writing is based on insights from previous warriors. That is the primary way God has designed His strategy to defeat His foe. If God is your Father, then we are family and we must help each other. What we have learned in regards to what works, and does not work, we must pass on to others! Share the ammunition! Share the wisdom you have learned from your victories as well as your defeats.

Relaxing is no more an option in this battle than playing tennis on a battlefield. Bullets are flying everywhere, and it is simply too dangerous to continue to play games. Casualties are dropping all around us and we should attempt to help the wounded. We must invest in our families to help prepare them to stand strong when they leave the safety of our homes. We must reach out to our brothers and sisters in Christ and help in any way we can.

Researchers like George Barna tell us that Christian marriages are breaking up at the same rate as the non-Christians'. Teenagers from godly homes are virtually no different from their unsaved friends in the behavioral choices they make. We must fight back, and we need to begin now! Whatever age you are, and no matter how far you may have fallen, if you are on the path to purity, you have a responsibility to help those God places in your life. Whatever helpful tools you use, share them with anyone who will listen, especially those in your own home.

The apostle Paul challenged those whom he influenced to follow his example and to imitate his lifestyle. As believers in the Lord Jesus Christ, we should do the same, especially in the arena of moral purity. Paul states it clearly:

> *But among you there must not be even a hint of sexual immorality, or of any kind of impurity, or of greed, because these are improper for God's holy people. (Ephesians 5:3)*

Are there any hints in our life of sexual immorality, or any kind of impurity? If someone walked around and recorded our words and activities during a typical day, what picture would be formed? If our thoughts could be known to everyone around us, would we have to change them? Once we are morally free, once we gain even a measure of freedom in our thought lives, we must be on guard never to go back to a sensual lifestyle. Can we, will we, say to those who are examining our lives, "Follow me" or "Imitate me"? At least we can say, "Learn from my failures, and do not imitate them." If we cannot, or will not, say, "Imitate me," why not? Is there willful sin that we refuse to release? What is keeping us from walking in purity? Do we feel like such failures that we have nothing of value to share?

Sometimes I do, and then I remember a story I read one time. The tale begins with a man who was hopelessly lost in a large forest. As he wandered around for days, he realized that he was completely lost and confused. All of the many paths looked just alike, and each one he chose led back to the same spot. After a few more days, he encountered another man who was obviously lost as well. This unshaven man in filthy clothes greeted him with a smile and offered to help. The first man huffed, "How can you help me when you are as lost as I am?" The other man winked and said, "True, I am lost, but I know over a hundred paths that do *not* lead out of the forest!" How many "paths" do you and I know that do not lead out of the forest of lust and entrapment? We can help others regardless of our failures and, many times, specifically *because* of them. Each failure is not a waste if, and it is a big if, we learn something of value from that defeat. We can assist others by sharing our own defeats and struggles. More importantly, we can help others by sharing what we learned from failure, and how we eventually overcame it.

Begin today, right now. God has already placed around you those who need your help. If you are male, other men need your assistance to overcome the sexual attacks they are suffering, so share what you have learned that works, and what does not. Why not ask a few men to meet with you weekly for a cup of coffee. Use the study guide in the back of this book and talk. Maybe, just maybe you could be used of God to save a marriage or help keep a brother from becoming just another statistic.

If you are female, there are women young and old whom you can instruct by your example and words. The same is true for children and teenagers. It is never too early to gain the upper hand in the battle for moral purity, and battles won while young will produce a lifetime of good fruit. In fact, Paul encourages the young people with these words:

> *Let no one despise you for your youth, but set the believers an example in speech, in conduct, in love, in faith, in purity.* 1 Timothy 4:12

Young men and women can set an example and should. Consider how you speak, how you live your daily lives, how you walk in love, faith and purity. What would happen to our churches and this nation if a groundswell of young men and women began to walk this way? Can you picture with me an army of pure, godly soldiers invading the kingdom of darkness with holy light? I pray we live long enough to find out. Will you join them?

When facing your next moment of temptation, ask the Holy Spirit to give you wisdom and grace to be obedient. Quote scripture and pray for others. God desires to set you free and He will give you the victory over sin, if you simply ask Him for it. As you gain strength and victory in this arena, ask God to bring people into your life that *you* can help. Then, be available to meet and pray with them as they request. Your life has a purpose, and at least part of that purpose is to assist others. Even our mistakes and failures serve as warnings and examples to others, so do not allow your experiences to be wasted by your silence. God does not squander anything that we commit to Him, including our failures. If everyone who reads this learns how to possess our "vessel" in purity and holiness, we will then be able to assist others in this constant war for moral purity.

I pray the church awakes, and that we will not only survive the current battle but begin to go on the offensive! I pray we begin to beat back the flood of perversion that is attempting to sweep away our families and the church. Christian men, women, boys, and girls must resist our sensual world system, and seek purity, holiness, and moral victory. Our families, churches, and our culture hang in the balance, awaiting our choices. We must not fail! Rise up and let us begin to change our world one person at a time for God's glory.

We must begin at home, then church, our workplaces, our neighborhoods, and wherever else God may lead. May God set us free in the realm of moral purity to be pure, bright lights bringing hope through Christ to our darkened world!

Courage to Flee: Study Guide

Questions seem to open up a new way of thinking. As we ponder something, say a problem, task or challenge, asking questions always forces us to explore concepts and solutions we may have ignored. Sometimes it is helpful to sit and just think deeply about a situation. In the old days reporters were taught to ask who, what, where, when and why questions, to make sure they covered all the bases. It would not hurt us at all to do the same regarding the topic covered in this book.

After asking ourselves questions about a situation, discussion with others will reveal multiple perspectives. No two people are exactly alike and all of us come at issues from a unique point of view. Studying this book in a small group of men or women is highly encouraged. Due to the nature of the discussion, I would recommend men or women only groups.

Each chapter is short and saturated with Scripture. By gathering in a small group to discuss the concepts covered in the chapter, you will find strength and accountability to pursue your goal of freedom.

If we really want to be free, then we will do whatever is necessary to throw off what entraps us. Until we want our freedom more than the enjoyment of our sin, we will remain entangled. Sin is pleasurable for a season, but the Bible teaches that the wages of sin are death. One sure fact is that those wages are always paid.

You have taken a good first step by reading the book. As you ask questions and share what you are learning with others, the truth of God's Word will further penetrate into your heart. God wants us to be free in Him. He desires us to worship Him in spirit and truth. Once we come out of the darkness we will see much clearer.

We can walk in moral purity. We can find forgiveness for our failures. We are dearly beloved children of the King. As you pray, ask questions, and discuss these chapters together with others, I pray the Lord will bring a freedom you only have dreamed of.

Dr. Jeff Klick

Introduction:

Marriage is a gift from God. The union physically, emotionally and mentally that can take place makes this earthly relationship the best one available to us this side of heaven. But, even with a wonderful marriage, a satisfying physical relationship, and excellent communication, moral failure still runs rampant in Christian homes.

Personal Reflection:

If married, am I satisfied in my marriage?

What one thing could I do to change my feelings about my marriage?

Am I morally free or bound up in some area?

What do I really want from this study?

Group Discussion:

1. Each of us that know Jesus as our Lord and Savior has a starting point in our walk with God. What's yours? Share how you came to know Christ.

2. Once we are born again, everything begins to change. Does it seem like we start fast after our initial conversion, then slow down or actually go backwards? Why is that?

3. Why do so many men and women in ministry fail morally? Why did so many great men in the Bible fail morally?

4. Do you think God made a mistake when He created us with such strong sexual drives? If you were God would you have created us this way? Why?

5. Why is marriage not all that is needed in learning how to control our sexual drives?

Chapter 1. The Slippery Slope of Compromise:

Each day we are heading somewhere. Every minute of every day we are doing something. What we do, how we think, and what action we take based on those choices, determines where we will end up when our day is over. The interaction between a man and a woman is a wonderful gift from God. Sadly, much of this gift from our Father has been perverted. We would be wise to be aware of the way we are wired as male and female humans and act accordingly in the moral arena.

Personal Reflection:

Am I involved in a relationship that is leading me up the oil-covered hill?

Am I attracted to someone of the opposite sex who is not my spouse?

Am I involved in anything that would bring embarrassment if discovered by others?

Am I spending time with someone other than my spouse and enjoying it in an improper way?

Have I made any little compromises that will lead to a big disaster?

Am I ready to flee for the sake of my family and my relationship with God?

Group Discussion:

1. Do you agree or disagree with Dr. Klick when he states that he does not believe that someone simply falls into adultery or addiction? Is all sin preceded by thinking? Why or why not?

2. Why would Paul tell us to flee from sexual immorality when we are told to stand and fight in other places? What about will power and grace from God, can't we just resist temptation here and the devil will flee from us?

3. Is it wrong for a man to have a relationship with a woman or visa-a-versa who is not their spouse? How close of a relationship should it be? Is Dr. Klick over reacting when he addresses this issue?

4. What are your feelings about the arts and long term, close interacting between the genders? Do you agree with Dr. Klick about the dangers of these activities? What could be done to help limit these risks?

5. What is so dangerous about compromise? Why do we always seem to go further than we intended? What could we do differently to help avoid compromise?

Chapter 2 - We Do What We Think:

The Bible speaks a great deal about taking our thoughts captive to Christ and to having our minds renewed. We are also told to be aware of schemes of our enemy and to make sure we are not taken captive by his deceptions. There seems to be a great warfare for our souls that takes place between our ears.

Personal Reflection:

If thinking precedes action, where are my thoughts taking me?

What do I allow my mind to dwell upon throughout the day?

Would my thoughts be able to pass through the Philippians 4:8 filter?

Would I have to change my thoughts if others could "hear" them?

Am I rationalizing anything specifically regarding escaping my marriage?

Group Discussion:

1. What does Paul mean by not being conformed to the world but be transformed by the renewal of our minds? What does Paul mean by testing and discerning in Romans 12:2?

2. Do you think Jesus was really tempted with lust? Why or why not?

3. The human mind is capable of rationalization and mankind has been able to justify just about anything. Are these two processes a gift or a curse? Why?

4. Consider the four examples of rationalization given in the chapter. Rank them in terms of destruction and then in terms of ease of believing. Explain why.

5. Is it really possible to live our lives through the Philippians 4:8 filter that Dr. Klick mentions? How would we go about doing that in our day to day lives? What impact would this have in our viewing, talking, entertainment choices, etc?

Chapter 3 - The Eyes are the Window to the Soul:

We really don't have a great deal of control over what comes into our line of sight. However, we have a choice over what we do next. If someone just watched our eyes all day long what would be revealed by what we look at?

Personal Reflection:

Am I careful about what I allow my eyes to feast upon and for how long they look?

Am I aware of the tug of the surrounding culture to lure me into moral failure?

Am I practicing the "law of second glance"?

How is the light in me—bright and shining, or dim and getting darker?

Group Discussion:

1. A marketing guru friend of mine is fond of saying, "the average American receives over 20,000 marketing messages a day." I am not sure of the actual amount, but I would venture to say many of those messages are saturated with sensuality. Why is that do you think? Is it simply a marketing ploy or something worse?

2. Do you agree with Dr. Klick's observations about weddings and women's fashions? How much of her body should a woman of God expose to every man that looks at her? Why?

3. What about the "Law of second glance" that Dr. Klick explained? Do you agree with it? Do you think it is helpful? Is it possible to stare at someone of the opposite sex and just enjoy the view without crossing over any dangerous lines? Why or why not?

4. Some people believe that you can actually see light or darkness in another's eyes. Do you believe that? Is there anything to that concept? Are they referring to actual light and darkness or something else? How would you explain that concept to someone?

5. What do you think Jesus meant with His comments in Matthew 6:22-23? How can light be darkness? Are there degrees of light and darkness then? Why?

Chapter 4 - Help for the Entangled: How Do I Escape?

When we are really ready to be free, we can break the chains that bind us. We can find accountability and help when we grow to the place where we hate our sin more than we love the pleasure received from it. If we could see sin from heaven's point of view, I wonder if we would react differently?

Personal Reflection:

Am I trapped, or heading for a trap, in an immoral relationship?

Do I really want freedom from sexual sin?

Am I willing to starve and cut off whatever is feeding it in my life?

Have I believed the lie that no one is hurt by my behavior?

Have I repented like King David?

Am I involved in any behavior that will increase the temptations in my life?

Have I given the devil a place in my life to build his camp?

Who would be a good prayer target?

Group Discussion:

1. Why is it so hard to keep the promises we make to God?

2. What techniques in addition to the starvation one Dr. Klick mentions, could be used to help gain freedom from moral failure?

3. Why did King David say he sinned against God and Him alone? What about Bathsheba and her husband? What about the faithful subjects who followed him?

4. Why is confession such a necessary part of forgiveness and restoration? Give examples.

5. Do you agree or disagree with Dr. Klick regarding dancing, hanging out at bars and clubs, etc.? Why or why not? What about prayer targets, would this really help in our battle?

Chapter 5 - Yes, Cain, We are our Brothers' (and Sisters') Keepers!

When confronted with his sin, Cain asked if he was really responsible. The answer is yes. While we have no control over what others think or do, we still have personal responsibility over our behavior. We must examine it in light of someone's point of view or vision.

Personal Reflection:

When I stand in front of a mirror, what part of my body am I attempting to highlight?
What are my motives in how I wear my clothes?
What are my motives in the way I conduct my conversations with others?
Am I attempting to help those of the opposite sex or trap them?
Do I have their best interests in mind or my own?
Have I been influenced by the world's way of dressing and acting in any fashion (pun intended)?

Group Discussion:

1. Are the fashion designers and trend setters of our world for or against moral purity? Why do you think so? Does it matter what their motives may be?

2. Where should the line be drawn regarding modesty? Why do you think so? What do you interact with those who do not draw the line at the same place?

3. Do you agree or disagree with Dr. Klick about the usage of terms like, "hot" "sexy" "available" etc. on clothing? How about this in referring to a brother or sister in Christ?

4. What about men and modesty? Does it matter how a woman dresses or is it all just a man's problem? What about flirtation, can it be just as tempting as immodesty is? Why?

5. How does being modest or non-flirty fit into esteeming others as better than you? Are we really supposed to be that concerned with one another? Why or why not?

Chapter 6 - Parents: Start Early, Interfere Often:

In order to know how your children are really doing you must spend sufficient time with them. Their behavior must be observed to see if they are really implementing or even understanding your instructions. Children grow quickly and we only have a small window to train. Once it is gone, it is too late.

Personal Reflection:

Am I investing enough time in the supervision of my children?

Do I "know well the condition of my flock"?

Am I willing or prepared to discuss sexuality with my children?

Do I know who their friends are?

Am I aware of any emotional bonding that they may be experiencing?

Have I observed how my wife and daughters are dressing from a man's point of view? How about my son's behavior towards girls?

Are my children involved in a potentially dangerous relationship with the opposite sex?

Group Discussion:

1. How important is it for a parent to supervise their children? If the children are with other good kids, does it really matter? Why or why not?

2. At what age should a parent let go of their children? Explain why? Are we being influenced by the culture or the Scripture with our answer?

3. What is the proper age for children to become involved with someone of the opposite sex? Why?

4. Should children have personal emails, FaceBook, passwords, texts, and other social media outlets that are off limits to parents? Why or why not?

5. Has the Church taken on the standards of the world around Her? Why or why not? How would we know?

Chapter 7 - Is There Hope For Those Who Have Failed?

There was only one perfect man, and that was Christ. All the rest of us live in various stages of failure by comparison. While not an excuse for sin, it certainly explains why we fall. The issue is not so much the failure, but the redemption available after the fall. Jesus forever lives to make intercession for us, and to redeem us.

Personal Reflection:

Do you understand God's forgiveness and His redemptive power personally?

If you have failed in this area, what would you tell others to help them avoid the same mistakes you have made?

Has God placed anyone in your life that you could assist in this battle?

Could you help in your church in some way to be of assistance to those trapped in sexual sin?

Are you training your children to be aware of the battle?

Group Discussion:

1. We all fall and fail, so why do we spend so much time being surprised at it when it happens? Why is it so easy to see the failures in others and so hard sometimes to see it in ourselves?

2. What does it mean to you that you are God's workmanship? Why do we not feel like a masterpiece in process?

3. Why is so hard to confess our sins to each other, and even to God when He stands ready to forgive us so freely?

4. What is the difference between guilt and shame? Between conviction and condemnation? Why is it so hard to discern between the two sometimes?

5. Should leaders be held to a higher standard of behavior? Is that fair? Why or why not?

Chapter 8 - Be On Your Guard - Always!

It is very easy to slip and fall if we are not careful. If we really had a true glimpse of the warfare going on all around us, I wonder if we would live differently that we do. Dropping our guards is easy but recovery from a knockout punch is not. We must remain diligent if we hope to succeed.

Personal Reflection:

Am I having a daily, growing relationship with God?

Am I drifting in any arena?

Am I swimming alone in dangerous waters without any support system in place?

Am I taking the necessary precautions with the Internet, TV, and anywhere I spend my time?

Am I being careful enough with my interactions concerning the opposite sex?

Am I involved in any compromising relationship, or even presenting the appearance of one?

Have I set up the necessarily guidelines to deal with sexual temptation before the battle begins?

What one thing could I do better than I am doing now to help in this war?

Group Discussion:

1. What is the difference between being tempted and sinning? Where do we draw the line in our minds? Can we?

2. If drifting is as dangerous as Dr. Klick states, how do we keep from doing so?

3. Why is community so important in our walk with God? How do we know if we are becoming isolated?

4. What would you say to someone if they asked you to violate your personal convictions regarding male and female relationships? How would you explain your stance?

5. Discuss some of the techniques Dr. Klick shared in this chapter such as open doors, frontal hugs, riding alone with someone of the opposite who is not your spouse, holding hands, etc. Do you agree with these? What others would you add?

Chapter 9 - The Goal of Freedom:

Do we live our lives with an eternal purpose in mind? Would we be willing to endure suffering if we knew God would use it someday to really help another person?

Personal Reflection:

Am I actively seeking out others that I may assist in some fashion?

Am I willing to be honest about my failures in order to help someone else with theirs?

Is there any hint of sexual immorality in my life?

Is there any area of my life that I have not cleansed or examined?

If I have fallen, will I get back up and try again?

Is there anything that I need to repent of concerning impurity?

Have I given thanks to God for the moral purity that I now have?

Group Discussion:

1. Have you ever been able to help someone else by sharing your failures? Share if you are comfortable enough.

2. How is our life like living in a warzone? What would we need to change if we really did see bullets flying around?

3. If someone could read our thoughts, or if they were displayed on a monitor on our chests for the entire world to see, would we need to change something? Explain.

4. Are we challenging the young men and women in the Church to meet the high expectations of 1 Timothy 4:12? Why or why not?

5. Do you believe there really is hope for the Church? For you? For victory over sexual sin? Why or why not?

I trust these questions at both the personal and group level have been helpful to your quest for moral purity. Please do not give in or up! God is not finished with any of us yet. If you have enjoyed this book, then please pass it on to someone else. May God get the glory for any freedom gained!

Dr. Jeff Klick

www.jeffklick.com

Appendix

Helpful Books and Websites:

Christian Modesty and the Public Undressing of America—Jeff Pollard, Chapel Library

What the Bible Says About Child Training—R. Fugate, Foundation for Biblical Research

What the Bible Says About Being a Man—Richard Fugate,

Discovering the Mind of a Woman—Ken Nair, Thomas Nelson Publishers

www.kids-in-mind.com—rates movies in violence, sexual content, and language

www.pluggedinonline.com/movie—provided by Focus on the Family

www.preview.gospelcom.net/—Family-based movie reviews

www.c4fic.org/—Family-based seminars and articles

www.hopefamilyfellowship.org - my church's website

Articles of Interest:

An Open Letter to the Sisters in the Body of Christ (please feel free to copy and give away if you desire.)

Christian Sensuality

The Formerly's

The Story of Beth

A Partial Listing of Applicable Scriptures

Biography

Courage to Flee

The following is an anonymous letter that we hand out in our church. Several other pastors use it as well—It is an appeal for the Christian sisters (and their fathers and husbands) to think about their brothers in the Lord before they come to worship.

To My Christian Sisters in the Body of Christ,

I am a brother in the Lord who wants to appeal to you for help. I love the Lord and desire to please Him in every way, including my thought life. I also represent many other brothers who wish they could write this to you but just cannot find the words.

We men are in a battle for our minds and hearts daily. This world system assaults our eyes and mind with pictures, music, entertainment, and words that attack our goal of moral purity. Everywhere we turn, there are images that appeal to the sensual flesh and sexual drive. Beautiful women are used to sell and promote everything. Like Job, we have tried to make a covenant with our eyes that we will not sin against God, (Job 31:1) but it is becoming increasingly more difficult. The devil has stepped up his attack to cripple us men through temptation and wandering eyes.

My appeal to you sisters is for an oasis in the church. It is one thing to struggle daily in the world, it is quite another to have to do battle in the church. We desire to attend church to worship and be strengthened at God's house, and we hope for at least a pause in the battle with lust and compromise. The world's system has crept into and is trying to corrupt the church on every front: selfish leaders, worldly music and entertainment, and now even sensual and seductive dressing by the sisters of all ages. Our enemy is sometimes using your fashion choices and you might not be aware of it.

God has designed men to be attracted by what they see. When a sister wears tight-fitting, slinky, clingy clothes, short skirts, or sleeveless outfits, it is a struggle! Eyes are drawn to what is highlighted on your body. Necklines that are low, or shirts unbuttoned, hems that are high, inappropriately placed broaches and necklaces all point to areas that we do not want to focus on! These things can draw the eye to places they should not be.

Age, weight, height, and other physical features do not really matter. The devil is using inappropriate dressing to cause brothers, young and old alike, to have to wage war even during worship! We attend church to worship our Lord, and often end up leaving frustrated and defeated. Please help us! Please take a moment and think about what you are going to wear. Where will someone's eyes go when they look at you? What part of your body do you really want men to look at? Shouldn't it be the face and eyes? Let us have a few minutes away from temptation and struggles. Let us have a time of refreshment and peace in the House of the Lord.

I am not asking you to wear burlap bags, but only modest, loose fitting clothing that does not highlight and accentuate your figures. Please draw attention to your eyes and smile instead of your chest or body. We are not lust-crazed animals, but men of God who desire to walk with you as sisters, and not have to struggle with you as a temptation.

Courage to Flee

We will continue to do battle on our end with our thought life; please assist us in our struggle by highlighting your face and not your body. Thanks for hearing our cry, and to God be the glory.

A Struggling Man Of God On Behalf Of My Brothers In Christ

Christian Sensuality

I don't get it. Why is it that Christian men and women feel the need to be sensual, seductive, half dressed, and look like they want to jump into bed with anyone and everyone? From FaceBook to Pinterest, Twitter to Instagram, Christians pose in slinky clothes, fashion model like poses, and everyone applauds them. Why? Why is it that if someone (male or female) shows cleavage, thigh, rippled abs, skin tight clothes highlighting their private parts, everyone uses words like, beautiful, lovely, gorgeous, stud, hot, etc. instead of words like, shameful, seductive, provocative, sensual, and stumbling material? Where has our discernment gone? Have we forgotten how to blush?

In the effort to avoid the dreaded word, "legalism," have we swung so far over to license? Don't we have a responsibility to present our temples (bodies) in a holy, modest way? Is Hollywood setting the standard of modesty instead of the Church? Why do we have to go sensual and bear our bodies to be considered attractive and lovely?

The Scripture states clearly that beauty should come from within, not from highlighting our bodies:

1 Peter 3:3-5 - Do not let your adorning be external—the braiding of hair and the putting on of gold jewelry, or the clothing you wear— but let your adorning be the hidden person of the heart with the imperishable beauty of a gentle and quiet spirit, which in God's sight is very

precious. For this is how the holy women who hoped in God used to adorn themselves, by submitting to their own husbands. (ESV)

Why shouldn't our clothes point to our faces instead of other parts of the body? With the proliferation of porn, the destruction of marriage through sexual immorality, and addictions running rampant, why isn't the Church rebelling against these trends? I ask again, have we lost our discernment?

Solomon warned his sons, and us, to avoid the harlot or sensual, seductive, woman (or man). Consider this passage for just a moment:

Proverbs 7:10 - And behold, the woman meets him, dressed as a prostitute, wily of heart. (ESV)

There are many aspects to consider here, but one clear one is that the woman was dressed in such a way as to communicate that she was available for hire. Our clothing matters and speaks to reveal our intentions. Shouldn't we, as ambassadors for Christ, living epistles known and read by all men, consider what we are saying with what we are wearing?

There is another disturbing trend arising over the last decade or so. Young couples court or date, attempt to remain sexually pure, and then marry. Almost as soon as saying "I do," the husband begins to demand that his wife change. He asks her to be more seductive, show more skin, and be sexier. Get tattooed, pierced, show cleavage, shorten the dresses or shorts, and act more sensual. As if to show off his trophy, the man demands that his wife move towards sensuality. Instead of protecting and cherishing his bride, the husband instills in her the seeds of destruction that will bloom sooner than later.

In addition, for some reason some guys now think that porn is ok. Bring the porn into the bedroom and let's play porn stars. Get kinky, weird, stretch the boundaries of propriety and demean the girl for not readily being willing to throw off moral restraint. The guy begins to mock and ridicule the standards that were initially attractive to him. We wonder why young married couples struggle to stay together long enough to turn into older couples in our day. Have we lost our discernment?

If we keep looking at the world for our acceptable standards we are in deep trouble. The Scripture should be our standard of behavior and thinking patterns. As long as we continue to imitate the nations around us, we are not going to be an effective light to them. If we look like, act like, think like, and respond just like the world, we will not be successful in changing it.

Sensuality arises from the heart. When we are posing, dressing, and wanting others to look at us, what are we really thinking at that moment? Are we bringing glory to God with how we look and act or are we somewhere else? What is our motive for our behavior? I believe we need a serious heart change if we ever expect to make a real difference in our world.

Paul challenged his readers with this thought:

Ephesians 5:3 - But among you there must not be even a hint of sexual immorality, or of any kind of impurity, or of greed, because these are improper for God's holy people. (NIV)

When we are exposing, highlighting, or drawing attention to the private parts of our bodies, are we really obeying this verse? When we are demanding that our spouses show more, highlight their bodies, be sexier, hot, or whatever the latest word is, are we pushing the boundaries of proper behavior? Have we lost our discernment? Have we forgotten how to blush?

Finally, I know the comments, arguments, justifications, and responses that could be sent to me, for I have heard them all before. "The guys have the problem. (True) They need to quit looking with lust. (True) I'm free in Christ. (True, with restraints based in love) What do you want me to wear, a bag or something? (No, just consider others as more important than yourself in how you dress) You are trying to put me in bondage and you are a legalist," (Both untrue, legalism has to do with attempting to gain approval with God, and I am not even anywhere near that, I am simply asking you to think about what you are doing and why) and the list could go on.

My appeal is simply for us to ask the Lord if we have compromised or adapted to the culture around us in how we present our bodies to each other either in person or online. Are we walking in moral purity, really valuing others so as to not place a stumbling block in their way? Is there a "hint" of impurity, sensuality or immorality in how we look, act, speak, and conduct ourselves? Have we lost some of our discernment? I am just asking the questions, you are the one that must answer them between you and the Lord.

This is an article written in an attempt to help people realize that they are forgiven and new creations in Christ, and that young people can learn from the mistakes of their elders.

The Formerly's

Many of us are part of an exclusive group of people. Not the Illuminates, or Tri-laterals, but a group of people known as the Formerlys. We have secret pasts that we hide from almost everyone else. What people see today is often very different from what they would have seen in our pasts. The scripture has several of these lists—maybe you too are mentioned here.

As for you, you were dead in your transgressions and sins, in which you used to live when you followed the ways of this world and of the ruler of the kingdom of the air, the spirit who is now at work in those who are disobedient. All of us also lived among them at one time, gratifying the cravings of our sinful nature and following its desires and thoughts. Like the rest, we were by nature objects of wrath. (Ephesians 2:1–3)

Formerly, we were part of the "deads." We used to breath, eat, sleep, walk around, and act like those who were alive, but we were dead. When Adam sinned and ate the fruit, a death sentence was released on this earth, and all who are born are born dead. Many live their whole lives and do not even know it. There are still others who learn of it but do not really care. Those of us who are "Formerlys" were shocked to find this out and we wanted to exchange death for life!

Before life in Christ, we used to live following the ways of this world and we submitted to the ruler of the kingdom of the air—or Satan. "The spirit that is now at work in all of those who are disobedient"—Boy, if that does not describe our generation I do not know what does. All of us—Paul included—lived to gratify the cravings of our sinful nature, following the desire of its thoughts. "Formerlys" think a certain way. Their minds are in the process of being renewed. However, those who follow the spirit of disobedience that is working today think a very different way—almost every thought is selfish and disobedient to God's commands. These folks are controlled by their flesh and desires, and they are simply targets of wrath! God will judge those who refuse to join the elite group of folks called the "Formerlys."

Therefore, remember that formerly you who are Gentiles by birth and called "uncircumcised" by those who call themselves "the circumcision" (that done in the body by the hands of men)—remember that at that time you were separate from Christ, excluded from citizenship in Israel and foreigners to the covenants of the promise, without hope and without God in the world. But now in Christ Jesus you who once were far away have been

brought near through the blood of Christ. (Ephesians 2:11–13)

Remember who you were—separate from Christ, excluded from citizenship in Israel, and foreigners to the covenants of the promise—without hope and without God. What a mess we Formerly were; we are not to be controlled by our past, but we are to never forget it and we are to learn from it and not repeat it.

At one time we too were foolish, disobedient, deceived and enslaved by all kinds of passions and pleasures. We lived in malice and envy, being hated and hating one another. (Titus 3:3)

This is another take on the concept—we were foolish, disobedient, deceived, and enslaved by all kinds of passions and pleasures. Thinking we were free, boasting that we were able to do anything, we were actually slaves, deceived, and did not even know it! That is one of the problems of living in the darkness—we cannot really see what is real.

For you have spent enough time in the past doing what pagans choose to do—living in debauchery, lust, drunkenness, orgies, carousing and detestable idolatry. They think it strange that you do not plunge with them

into the same flood of dissipation, and they heap abuse on you. (1 Peter 4:3–4)

One thing that those who are deceived cannot stand is that there *are* "Formerlys." They want to drag these people of Light back into the darkness, for as long as they live in the Light, there is pressure and guilt. We Formerlys rarely have to say anything, for those of the darkness can see the difference, and they have either have a longing or a hatred that rises up with in them.

Why do I go through these verses? Two reasons, mainly:

1. We who are Formerlys need to know who we are now.

2. Many of our young folks have not had this experience of living in death, for most have grown up in Christian homes with strict guidance and control.

We will start with the second one first. I see a disturbing trend in the young people of today. Most of the children in our churches are "second generation" ones who have not lived an overt life of sin and wickedness. The control that has been put on them has not allowed them the opportunities that many of the non-Christian children have had to sin at will. So many of these young people cannot relate to the Formerlys. And, as the trend goes, many of these young folks are longing for the things that we Formerlys came out of—the bar scene, worldly music, flirtatious lives, and sensual gratification.

Oh, we Formerlys tell them that this stuff is bad. We explain that these choices will hurt them and scar them for life, but all too often they refuse to listen—and many even try the forbidden fruit. Like Eve, they see that it is lovely to look at and pleasant to the taste, but they don't see what we Formerlys see—death is there. We know, for we have come out of it. Therefore, many young church people are testing and trying the delights of the world. Now, God is faithful and His Word is true. Many prodigals will return and many of these young people will join the ranks of Formerlys soon enough. However, there will be scars and a great deal of pain and loss that could have been avoided. While grieving over the choices being made, we rest in the fact that our God is a redemptive God.

My appeal is for the young people to learn from the Formerlys and not get all scarred up. Experience may be the best teacher, but it is not the best way to learn biblically.

The first reason I mentioned was that we Formerlys know who we are now. We are children of the light. We no longer stumble around in the darkness. We are blood-washed forgiven children of the King. Former means that we are no longer what we were. We are now in the process of being changed into something wonderful. I can now look myself, the devil, and anyone else in the eye and say that I have been redeemed. I have been bought with a price. My sins and former way of life is dead and buried in Christ. It is no longer I who live but Christ Jesus who is living through me. I am a new creation in Christ. I do not do the same things I formerly did. I do not think the same way, act the same way, speak the same way, or desire the same things anymore. That old man is dead and buried and I do not want to go around digging up that old carcass. I study the Word of God and see that I just do not fit in this world system any more. The prince of the power of the air does not control me or have any say over me now. I used to serve him, but now I despise him and reject him. I do not do the things he wants me to do. I do not participate in the activities he sponsors. If all of his servants are speaking well of me, then I am probably doings some things I should not be doing.

Being a Formerly is a great privilege. Many are they who reject the offer and few are they who find it; we have a great salvation from a former way of living. We are forward-looking, not backward-looking. You and I have a glorious Hope in our Lord Jesus Christ. We must impart these truths to our children. Deuteronomy 6 tells us to talk to them about these things just about every waking moment.

If you are an adult and you are a Formerly, then you have a responsibility to live a life worthy of the calling you have received. If you are young, and maybe have not lived like the devil, you have a responsibility to listen to those who have and learn from their lives. The best testimony to me is from someone who has listened well to others and walked in the light his or her whole life. May we strive after the best!

This is a true story written by my daughter while she was in her twenties struggling with being single. I hope it warms your heart as it always does mine.

The Story of Beth
By: Sarah Klick (now Jansen)

I never met Beth. I do not even know her last name. But the Story of Beth gave me hope and encouraged me to keep walking down this path—this path of girlhood to womanhood, this path of desiring to stand alone for my convictions in singlehood.

It is not very romantic to celebrate another year in the twenties and not even have a boyfriend on the horizon. To force a smile through the tears as another one of your childhood girlfriends rides off into the sunset with her Knight in Shining Armor; to have the ring finger on your left hand still bare.

It is a struggle in this upside-down society to stick to the old-fashioned ideas that the guys are supposed to do the pursuing and wooing. The girls have books upon books, resources filling the shelves, reminding them that they are to wait patiently for the guys to win their hearts. Oh dear! Has anyone written anything reminding the guys of their responsibility? Do they know that they are supposed to be the conquerors and there are hearts to be won? Perhaps in all the confusion of equal rights for women, the guys have forgotten that there are some girls who hold fast to those obsolete ideas.

It is a struggle to be different, to have strong convictions and standards and guidelines. It is terrible to stand alone. To stand out and stand up when no one else is standing by your side. It is a challenge. It is an uncomfortable path to walk down.

Sometimes I wonder if it is worth it. Does anyone really notice? Does anyone really care? Does it really matter to any guy if a girl saves herself for him? If she dresses modestly? If she guards her heart and keeps herself pure? If she doesn't date and mess around with every guy of her acquaintance?

Are there any quality young men left out there? Or are all the guys attracted to the bare-legged, bare-chested, and bare-stomached; the tight mini-skirt, short shorts, low shirts, athletic-wear (which used to be called a bra—go figure) clad girls that show the world all that they are and more. Do guys really admire the aggressive types who woo and chase after them like they were their prey?

I was at my wit's end. Here I was, reminding myself to stand strong and walk in the direction I had chosen to follow—alone. Wondering if there were any quality young men waiting along the sidelines, or if they had already passed the finish line eons before me. I daily debated with myself if my standards were doing me any good. If there was any fruit whatsoever from them. If they even mattered. No one was knocking down my door; I did not even turn any heads. Such a lovely feeling to know that you are not desirable or what you hold up is not viewed as attractive or appealing. In my heart, I had reached the place that I was going to do what I thought was right, even though it meant being alone and rejected. I had to take some rough falls to develop this foundation—this mindset. But my mind was resolved. I was going to wipe my hands clean of the "hunting lioness act" and dump it all into God's hands and onto the guy's shoulders. If he wanted me badly enough, he would have to get up and do something about it. No more being Miss Available at the right time, and planting myself in the right position, and arranging "surprise bumping into each other." No more eye contact to get my interest across. No more information-loaded comments thrown into the air and pairing off. I was tired of doing all the work and I was not at all pleased with the fruits of my labor. If the "old fashioned" idea of the girls being sought after, wooed, and won, worked back then, why could it not work now? Why should I throw myself at someone and put so much effort into it if he does not even want me? Why waste time, energy, and emotion when I do not even know if he cares? Maybe he does not even know we are on the same planet or I am the *last girl in the world he would ever marry?*

It would seem backwards to me if I should get down on my knee and propose to him, so why shouldn't it seem backwards to me to do all the prerequisite work that leads up to the Big Question? So much thought for food ☺

It was a hot July afternoon. My younger (but taller! and very mature) brother David and I were taking a walk on the peaceful little trail up the street from our house. Our favorite times to talk together, really talk about anything and everything, always seemed to be during our walks outside, as we journeyed through the wooded trail enjoying the sounds of the birds and scampering of squirrels.

139

I remember that we were crossing under some overhanging trees, taking advantage of the few moments of shade, when David suddenly asked me, "Have I told you about Beth?" He had been gone traveling for several months and had met so many new people and been to so many new places, he had enough stories to share for a lifetime. My eyebrows rose at the mention of a strange girl's name coming from my brother's lips. I wondered what she was to him and if he was about to tell me about my sister-in-law to be. The suspicion must have been written all over my face, because David smirked and a twinkle came into his eye. He loved to stir up my protective, big sister emotions. "No," I said, "I don't believe that you've ever mentioned Beth." I waited to hear her story. I do not know what I was expecting. Another girl who made eyes at my big, handsome brother, maneuvered and manipulated the situation so they could get to know each other. I had seen it done before. I had done it myself. I was sick of all the guy-girl stuff, all the games and playing around. Now some Beth girl had entered the scene—I hoped she was a girl worth fighting for.

David raised his hands defensively; "It's nothing like that, Sarah. Come on. Let me tell you about Beth." I bit my tongue to fight back the questions threatening to tumble out. "Okay, David, I'm listening. Tell me about Beth."

David drifted into reverie. "We were out in California working at a camp, learning how to work with river rescuing. A Christian camp shared the river with another non-Christian camp. There were teenagers everywhere. All the girls looked like clones.

They had on the short shorts and the spaghetti-strap shirts, if you can call them shirts. The river was the worst place to be, with all the girls swimming in their bikinis and their immodest bathing suits. The other guys and me were having a hard time keeping a guard over our eyes—everywhere we turned, there were half-naked girls, giggling and flirting and showing off their bodies.

"One day, we met a girl who seemed to have a different spirit about her. She was friendly and had a beautiful warm smile, along with sparkling bright eyes. We immediately felt comfortable with her. She and her sister worked at the camp across the river. Her sister was going to be out on the river tomorrow the same time we were. Her sister's name was Beth. We were anxious to meet her. If she was anything like her older sister, she just might be a quality young woman—and about our own age!

"We were not disappointed. Beth stood out on the river that day from every other girl there, and all the guys in my unit noticed with respect and awe. She wore shorts over her swimming suit, along with her life jacket. She was not out there to draw attention to her body—in fact; she went to great lengths to keep herself covered. And she wasn't flirty with the guys, just friendly.

"That evening, she sat with our group at the dinner table, once again dressed modestly—wearing longer shorts than any other girl did at camp, and we got to talk with her and observe her. She radiated with God's love, and His spirit shone in her eyes. She greatly impressed every guy at my table. She was the topic of conversation from then on. Every guy stated that he wanted to marry a girl like

Beth, someone who went against the flow and was pure and unstained by the world. She lived right in the middle of all the worldly influence, yet was stronger than its pull. She worked at a camp where she was daily surrounded by girls who did not share her convictions and probably made fun of her for them. She chose to be different. To dress different. To take a stand—alone."

I never met Beth. I do not even know her last name. But nine young men who saw that she was a quality woman of God in a perverse and lost world admired Beth. They saw the difference in her appearance and her lifestyle. She loved the Lord. Period. And, her life was a reflection. She wanted to dress modestly. She did not care if she was the only one and if all the girls thought she was an old fogy. She wanted to honor God with her body and not be a stumbling block for the guys who crossed her path. I do not doubt for a second that it was difficult for her—maybe putting on those shorts over her swimming suit was the most challenging part of her day. Maybe she had to talk herself through every step, reminding herself that there was a bigger picture she could not see. Maybe, in her heart, she longed to be "normal" and fit in. I do not know. I will never know. But, because she was different, because she did choose to dress modestly and act like an honorable Christian young lady, she made a lasting impression.

She did draw attention to herself by her choices, the attention of some quality young men who noticed the contrasting difference in her compared to the other hundreds of other girls before their eyes. David had so much respect for Beth. He knew that it took a lot of strength to stand alone. He admired her for it, and was convicted by it.

As we walked along, both thinking about Beth, David began to tell me how important it was to him to find a "Beth." The other girls are a dime a dozen. They look, talk, dress, flip their hair, and walk the same. They use the same flirting moves and seductive traps. They do not have any backbone to be different—or the heart or desire for the things of the Lord. Their eyes are on what the world is dangling before them. They are snared, and are eager to snare others. Beth's walk matched her talk. She was like a twinkling star surrounded by millions of planets in the night sky. She was a rare and precious jewel. She probably does not even know how her actions influenced others. How she set an example and inspired some young men to keep their standards high when it came to looking for a girlfriend.

There was only one Beth at that camp in California (along with her sister)—what a tragic thing. Only one girl who was walking down the path less traveled on. One girl who set some guys seriously contemplating what is important, and what they long for. It is not easy to be a Beth, but I am so thankful for the lesson she taught my brother and me. She taught me to keep my eyes focused on the goal and not to give up hope. The price is high, but the result is worth it. It does not matter if you are completely alone; keep on walking. Keep on shining like a star in a crooked and perverse generation.

She taught David that there are important things to be desired in a wife. And, the most crucial, her love and devotion to the Lord, far outweighs the pressure from her peers, or the pressure from the world, or even the pressure from other sisters in the Body of Christ. We are called to be a holy and peculiar people, a people who are in the world but not of it. A people who are different and who are a light in the dark world. How can they see our light if we hide it under a bowl? How can we stand out if we are not standing up? Beth stood alone and made a lasting impact. I hope and pray that someday the Story of Sarah will speak as much.

"Don't let anyone look down on you because you are young, but set an example for the believers in speech, in life, in love, in faith, and in purity." (1 Timothy 4:12)

Below is a partial listing of definitions and scriptures dealing with the topics of sexuality and sensuality.

Debauchery: Sensuality or lasciviousness, lewdness or shamelessness.

Immoral: Sometimes referred to as: Fornicator, whoremonger

Sensual: Seductive, immodest, attracting attention to the sexual parts of the body

Matthew 15:19
For out of the heart come evil thoughts, murder, adultery, sexual immorality, theft, false testimony, slander.

Acts 15:20
Instead we should write to them, telling them to abstain from food polluted by idols, from sexual immorality, from the meat of strangled animals and from blood.

Romans 13:13
Let us behave decently, as in the daytime, not in orgies and drunkenness, not in sexual immorality and debauchery, not in dissension and jealousy.

1 Corinthians 6:18
Flee from sexual immorality. All other sins a man commits are outside his body, but he who sins sexually sins against his own body.
1 Corinthians 6:9
Do you not know that the wicked will not inherit the kingdom of God? Do not be deceived: Neither the sexually immoral nor idolaters nor adulterers nor male prostitutes nor homosexual offenders

2 Corinthians 12:21

I am afraid that when I come again my God will humble me before you, and I will be grieved over many who have sinned earlier and have not repented of the impurity, sexual sin and debauchery in which they have indulged.

Galatians 5:19

The acts of the sinful nature are obvious: sexual immorality, impurity and debauchery;

Ephesians 4:19

Having lost all sensitivity, they have given themselves over to sensuality so as to indulge in every kind of impurity, with a continual lust for more.

Ephesians 5:3

But among you there must not be even a hint of sexual immorality, or of any kind of impurity, or of greed, because these are improper for God's holy people.

Ephesians 5:5

For of this you can be sure: No immoral, impure or greedy person—such a man is an idolater—has any inheritance in the kingdom of Christ and of God.

Ephesians 5:18

Do not get drunk on wine, which leads to debauchery. Instead, be filled with the Spirit.

Colossians 3:5

Put to death, therefore, whatever belongs to your earthly nature: sexual immorality, impurity, lust, evil desires and greed, which is idolatry.

1 Timothy 2:9

I also want women to dress modestly, with decency and propriety, not with braided hair or gold or pearls or expensive clothes,

Hebrews 12:16

See that no one is sexually immoral, or is godless like Esau, who for a single meal sold his inheritance rights as the oldest son.

1 Peter 4:3

For you have spent enough time in the past doing what pagans choose to do—living in debauchery, lust, drunkenness, orgies, carousing and detestable idolatry.

See also Proverbs 2, 5, 6, 7, 22, Revelation 21:8, 22.

For a deeper study, consider these:

Leviticus 18:1-30 – "You must not follow their practices."

Numbers 25:1-3 – "the men began to indulge in sexual immorality."

1 Samuel 2:22-25 "Eli's wicked sons."

1 Kings 11:1-10 – "Solomon loved many foreign women."

2 Kings 17:7-20 – "The reason Israel was carried into captivity."

Following the practices of the nations around Israel led to their downfall and captivity.

Romans 1:21-32 "God gave them over to their depravity."

1 Corinthians 5:1-13 "Sexual immorality among you."

1 Corinthians 6:9-20 "Flee sexual immorality."

2 Corinthians 12:20-21 "Not repented of their sexual sin."

Galatians 5:19-21 – "Deeds of the flesh are obvious."

Ephesians 4:17-19 – "No longer live like the Gentiles."

Ephesians 5:3-1-12 – "Not even a hint of sexual immorality."

Colossians 3:5-8 – "Put to death whatever…"

1 Thessalonians 4:1-8 "It is God's will…"

Titus 1:15-16 – "To the pure…"

Hebrews 12:14-17 – "See that no one is sexually immoral."

Hebrews 13:4 – "Marriage bed kept undefiled."

1 Peter 2:11-12 – "Abstain from fleshly lusts."

We are to be different from the world around us in all aspects. We are to be a holy people.

1 Corinthians 1:2 – "Called to be holy."

Ephesians 5:3 – "Improper for God's holy people."

Colossians 3:12 – "God's chosen people."

1 Thessalonians 2:12 – "Live a life worthy."

1 Thessalonians 4:7 – "Live a holy life."

1 Thessalonians 5:4-8 – "Sons of light."

1 Timothy 2:2 – "Live in godliness and holiness."

1 Timothy 4:11-12 – "Set an example."

1 Timothy 6:11 – "Pursue godliness and righteousness."

2 Timothy 1:9 – "Called us to a holy life."

2 Timothy 2:21-22 – "Flee evil and pursue righteousness."

Titus 1:8 – "Qualifications for leadership."

Hebrews 10:10 – "We've been made holy."

1 Peter 1:14-15 – "Do not conform to our evil past."

1 Peter 2:10-12 – "Live such good lives."

2 Peter 1:6 – "Make every effort."

2 Peter 3:1 – "Have wholesome thinking."

2 Peter 3:11-4 "Live godly lives, be holy and be found spotless."

Author's Biography

Dr. Jeff Klick has been in full time ministry for over thirty years and is the senior pastor at Hope Family Fellowship. Dr. Klick married his high school sweetheart, Leslie, in May of 1975. They have three adult children and ten grandchildren.

Dr. Klick loves to learn and has earned a professional designation, CFP, earned a Master's degree in Pastoral Ministry, a Doctorate in Biblical Studies, and a Ph.D. in Pastoral Ministry.

In addition to serving as senior pastor at Hope Family Fellowship, Dr. Klick is a consultant with The Institute for Church Management, a teaching Fellow with Christian Discipleship Ministries, part of the Pastor's Panel for the Alive in Christ Radio Show, Co-Host of Christian Business 360 Radio Show, serves on the Board of Directors for The Council for Family-Integrated Churches and is the president of Trinity Discipleship Institute. Dr. Klick writes a weekly blog, is a guest contributor to several websites, and has published multiple books.

For additional information on Dr. Klick's other books and ministry please visit: www.jeffklick.com